EXTRA MILE

Extra MILE

500 CUSTOMER SERVICE TIPS for SUCCESS

Tools to ATTRACT, SATISFY, & RETAIN Even the Most DIFFICULT CUSTOMER

TYCHO
PRESS

Contents

Introduction: Secrets of the Giants   **6**

PART 1
Customer Service
Overview **8**

PART 2
Customer Service
Basic Principles **18**

PART 3
General Rules **58**

PART 4
Real-Life Scenarios **97**

PART 5
Crisis Management **136**

PART 6
Building Customer
Loyalty **172**

PART 7
Customer Service Online **216**

PART 8
50 Things Never to
Do or Say **258**

References **310**

Index **319**

Introduction

SECRETS OF THE GIANTS

What is the secret to great customer service? From Apple to American Express, from Southwest to the Ritz-Carlton, top-service companies have studied their customers' needs and put them at the center of their corporate culture. Every one of their employees is ready to go out of her way to make the customer's experience the best it can be.

Now you can learn not only from these customer service giants but also from hundreds of smaller companies and their savvy consultants.

If you regularly interact with customers, *Extra Mile: 500 Customer Service Tips for Success* is the book for you. Whether you meet your clients face-to-face, work as an in-house customer service representative, or take inbound calls for a large corporation, you will benefit from our advice on how to deal with difficult people, sort out knotty situations, and handle awkward interactions with grace—making every customer glad she does business with you.

You will learn what to say when a customer calls up with an angry complaint or demands to talk to a supervisor. You'll discover how to defuse tension, and how to make her feel that you care about her predicament. You will learn the general rules for thinking about your business's customer service, and the many ways to listen to and empathize with clients while you work toward mutually beneficial solutions.

Extra Mile also explores some of the biggest mistakes made by real-world, high-visibility corporations, and the subsequent steps they took to make things right with their customers. In Part Five: Crisis Management, you will find advice on how to quickly recover from these kinds of scenarios—and some examples that may make you feel your crisis is not so bad after all.

HOW TO USE THIS BOOK

All companies offering great service will tell you that it takes much more than one trick to make every customer interaction great. That's why each part of *Extra Mile* contains up to 75 tips to help you refocus your approach. The tips are divided into several sections, so you can quickly find what you need. Headings like "Assuring" and "Acknowledging" help you with the nuts and bolts of talking to clients, while more specific ones like "Dealing with Angry Customers" and "Being Asked 'Why?' Repeatedly" guide you through more volatile situations.

The final part, "Fifty Things Never to Do or Say," gives you a quick reference guide to actions you should avoid at all costs if you want your customers to love your service.

Are you ready to go the extra mile and turn your organization's customer service into the engine that drives customer retention? Let's get started.

CUSTOMER SERVICE OVERVIEW

ere's a statistic that may open your eyes to the power of our social media–fueled society: Every day, American consumers have 2.4 billion conversations about brands. Some of them are talking about their favorite products, but the vast majority are telling stories about experiences they've had with a manufacturer or service provider—the company's willingness (or lack thereof) to solve a problem, its ability to make a bad situation right (or not), and the chances that they will or will not buy from that company again.

With so much talk out there, you won't be able to deal with every single message about your company. It's critical, then, that you keep a firm grasp on what you can control. At the top of that list is the service you provide your customers. If you make them happy, they will tell others about their great experience with you, and your business will grow. Equally important, these happy customers will continue to buy from you . . . and, again, your business will benefit.

Before the Internet changed the way in which we interact with customers, businesses could keep a fairly firm grasp on their relationships with them. Happy customers kept on buying, while unhappy customers would call a dedicated hotline, write a letter to the company, or grumble quietly to their friends and coworkers. They did not have the ability to broadcast their discontent to hundreds, thousands, or millions of people in a matter of minutes. The only failures in customer service that garnered regional or national attention were the truly spectacular ones: for instance, Ford and Firestone battling over which company bore the responsibility for defects that were causing Ford's sport utility vehicles to flip over. The conflict between these companies (see Part Five: Crisis Management) not only stripped them of their credibility for several years, but also distracted them from the need to do right by the victims of the faulty equipment—thus demonstrating their serious disregard for their clients.

Most companies' mistakes do not go as far. However, these days, a single person's account of a negative experience with your business can be equally destructive to your credibility.

In January 2014, professional musician Christopher Wilke was on his way home to Rochester, New York, from a performance in Salt Lake City. He was flying Delta Airlines. A renowned lute player, Wilke was traveling with a one-of-a-kind instrument: a 24-string baroque lute carefully handcrafted to replicate a German lute from 1754. Its monetary value was estimated at $10,000, but musicians—as any of them will tell you—tend to build a relationship with their instruments that transcends dollars and cents. In addition, Wilke maintained a brisk concert schedule, and needed this lute and its unique sound to make his living.

Wilke traveled with the lute as a carry-on item. When he changed planes in Detroit, however, the Delta staff at the gate informed him that the instrument was too big, and—ignoring his objections—stowed it in the baggage hold. When Wilke arrived at the airport in Rochester, he found the case cracked and his lute smashed. "Moments later, the tension from the strings on the broken instrument snapped off the sound board, sending splinters flying around the Delta baggage room," said a report of the incident in the *Rochester Democrat & Chronicle*. This took place in front of many witnesses.

What was the initial reaction of Delta's baggage claim attendant? First, she insisted that Wilke turn over his instrument so it could be shipped to a claims office—but she could not provide any information on where this office was, or how long the instrument would be gone. Wilke declined her offer . . . and as the gathering crowd became larger, the attendant panicked and announced that she was closing the baggage claim office altogether.

In the moments before this customer service rep started what would become a cascading system failure, Wilke took

A memorable phrase or smooth promise are no longer enough

photos of his smashed lute with his phone. Later that evening, he posted them on Facebook.

Refusing to leave the baggage office without a resolution, he demanded to see a supervisor, who suggested that he file a claim using a questionnaire that would be started in the office and completed online. This felt more comfortable for the musician, but when he got home and went to the Delta website to finish the process, he found that he had not been supplied with a file reference ID number. "When he called Delta, Wilke encountered a Catch-22 situation: He was told he couldn't get the file reference ID number because he didn't have a file reference ID number," the *Democrat & Chronicle* said. Then Wilke himself said, "I was told, 'There is no record of you having ever submitted a claim.'"

Luckily, he had a time- and date-stamped photo of the damage. It took him another two days to connect with someone at Delta who was willing to help him—but by then, his photos of his broken instrument had gone viral, along with his account of the incident. The classical-music world picked up the story, and others in the industry then began to pile on, telling stories of their expensive and valuable instruments also being trashed by the airline. Soon *USA Today* boosted the story's distribution to mainstream audiences. *Asia News* also posted it, thus taking the tale of Delta's epic failure to a worldwide audience.

Essentially, in *just two days*, the entire world had heard about Delta's shameful treatment of a young lute player, making it the airline to avoid for people carrying sensitive, fragile, or especially valued equipment of any kind.

Wilke did finally have his instrument repaired by the luthier who had originally built it, and Delta picked up the tab, reported to be about $3,000. The damage to the airline's reputation, however, will linger for years to come.

What can we learn from this story?

- The Internet has fundamentally changed more than the way people buy products. It has taken product-message control away from brand owners, and placed it in the hands of customers.

- The average citizen has more power than ever to retaliate if he or she does not receive good customer service.

- Customer service only *begins* with the buying decision— it continues through the entire life cycle of your product or service.

- Customer service must be a priority at every level of your organization.

- Never underestimate the power of the Internet to turn your company's small error into an image-killing, business-crushing disaster.

CUSTOMER SERVICE AND THE WHOLE PRODUCT

Even as we acknowledge the power of social media to link customers with products or services, let them express opinions about these products, and bring major brands to their knees, it's important that we not lose sight of the fundamental truths about product marketing and buying decisions. What may now be considered "old-school" thinking still tells us a great deal about the role customer service plays in the way people choose products—and the methods we can use to form lasting relationships with them.

A single person's account of a negative experience with your business can be destructive to your credibility

In his book *Crossing the Chasm*, Geoffrey Moore introduces the concept of the "whole product." He says a product is much more than the core object or service offered by a company—the whole product includes all the elements that make a customer want to buy it over others. These may include its warranty, the service contract or free customer service options, accessories or peripherals, manuals, training or classes, and access to online services, among others.

Customer service is one of the elements of the whole product, especially if you can develop a legendary offering. For example, one of the things that makes Apple's products so compelling—beyond their extraordinary capacity to remain ahead of the competition in terms of innovation and technology—is a user's ability to walk into an Apple store anywhere in the world and get free application and technical support from a "genius." This access is part of the promise Apple makes to its customers: Wherever you are, we are there to help you use our products better.

Most companies do not have Apple's resources, but you can still create a service offering that provides the kind of support your customers need. Whether that takes the form of 24-hour access to information and experts, a dedicated support person to answer questions, or an account executive who is empowered to make things right on the spot, you can offer a whole product that makes potential customers think seriously about choosing your company over your competition.

THE THREE STAGES
OF CUSTOMER SERVICE

As you begin to establish your company's ability to provide exemplary customer service, it's important to understand all the points at which your client engages with you. You can group these points into three stages: **acquisition**, **serving**, and **retention**.

Acquisition involves much more than the traditional sales call. In a world of online communications, the process of acquiring new customers largely takes place while you are not in personal contact with your target audience. According to research organization SAP, 57 percent of potential customers' decision-making process is completed before their first interaction with sales.

Customers seek their own information, basing their decisions not only on price but also on how well a product will solve their problem or serve their need. Once they have narrowed their choices down to a handful of products or service providers, they will base their final pick on their interaction with the companies.

In this book, we will focus on your and your staff members' ability to influence a customer's buying decision through your personal engagement with him. More than simple features-and-benefits selling, this acquisition process involves developing a sincere rapport with clients. These customers expect you to provide the answers they need to make a buying decision, prove you understand their wants and specific situation, and deliver on your promise of a quality product or service.

You need to understand your own customers and products, but you also need a working knowledge of your competitors' products. You will be expected to know what makes your product better than others on the market—especially if yours is more expensive.

Serving the customer is an ongoing process that involves a wide variety of activities. You are looking to build a long-term relationship by proving that your company is reliable, ready to solve problems as they arise, willing to help, and innovative in finding solutions.

If you manufacture a product, there will be times when it may not work. It will be up to you and your staff members to determine the cause of the problem, whether you can fix it with a phone call or a visit, and whether the product needs to be replaced. You will need to do this in a timely manner, making help available to your customers when they want it. Sometimes, even if the problem stems from their own mishandling, you will need to accept a return and replace the damaged or non-working item.

The way in which you take all these steps will leave your clients with a lasting, often permanent impression of your company. If you can handle their issues with grace and efficiency, you will build a rapport with them that will keep them coming back to your products. On the other hand, if you make their experience a chore, leave them with a broken or non-working product, or hire representatives who are incompetent or rude, you may send them out into the social media world with a juicy story that will drain away thousands of potential customers.

If your company provides a service (as opposed to selling a product), your clients expect open communication, updates on the progress of their projects, and strict adherence to timelines and schedules. They rightfully expect your project to come in on time and on budget, or to be told promptly if an addition or

It costs much less to retain a current customer than it does to go out and find a new one

Customer service is one of the elements of the whole product

change to its scope will cost them more money. While just about every project goes through some changes as it moves forward, this does not need to be a point of contention between you and your customer. If you are committed to providing great service, you can treat him as your partner in the process, and meet any new challenges together with him.

Retention is a result of the fine service you and your company provide. This kind of service helps build your customers' trust in you, and makes them eager to do business with you again. It also tells them that you care about their patronage, a key component in building a long-term relationship with them.

Just about anyone who owns a business knows that it costs much less to retain a current customer than it does to go out and find a new one. Maintaining your customer base not only stabilizes your profit potential and cash flow, but it also saves your company money in the long run.

Responding to clients' issues as they arise will help you keep them, but working proactively to find and prevent problems will raise your company to a whole new level. When you can keep your customers' projects from running off the rails, you demonstrate to them that you are thinking about their welfare even when they are not expecting you to do so. This is the kind of service that forms career-long relationships.

Your whole organization needs to make retention a driving factor in the way you deal with customers. Once you determine that you will do whatever is necessary (and legal) to keep the good ones, your service strategy must align with that goal.

Did you notice we said "good ones"? During the early stages of building your business, you may think that every customer who pays for your product or service is great. Over time, however, you will find that certain customers are simply not right for you. In Part Two, we will discuss how you can understand the qualities of your best clients, and how you can work to attract and keep others like them.

NO MORE SUCKERS

Entertainment syndicate leader David Hannum once said, "There's a sucker born every minute." He was referring to a scam perpetrated by another leader in entertainment, P. T. Barnum. When Hannum said this back in 1869, he was absolutely right. But today, when a quick and simple Google search or visit to Snopes.com can dispel a rumor or correct a misconception, you have a lot fewer suckers in your potential customer base.

Your customers can learn just about anything about your company and products, compare one product with another, read reviews from any number of amateur critics, decode the complex language of technological benefits, and take the words of frustrated buyers to heart. A memorable phrase or smooth promise are no longer enough to catch their favor; today, you and your company need to impress them not only with the quality of your products or the brilliance of your services, but also with your ability to deliver on every single promise you make.

It's time to acknowledge the level of self-acquired education every customer brings to the buying decision, and find ways to make your company and products stand out for him. Customer service can be one of the most potent differentiators. Through service, you can separate your company from your less motivated competitors.

PART

2

CUSTOMER SERVICE
BASIC PRINCIPLES

Let's start with some basics. Who is your customer, and how can you make her feel that buying your products or services is the right thing to do?

You're reading this book because you have a product or service to market. If your company is up and running, you already have a base of customers who have found your offering useful. If you're still in the formative stages, you have the opportunity to do some research before you begin selling.

Research plays a critical role in helping you identify the people and organizations in your target market. The more you know about who your customers are and why they need or want what you have to sell them, the better you will understand what elements of customer service will make a difference in their buying decisions.

This is a great time to go back to the basics of marketing and service, gather information, and set up the ground rules that will help your company form an enterprise-wide customer service approach.

Who Is Your Customer?

START WITH WHAT YOU'RE SELLING

Take a good look at your product offerings and build a clear picture of the market you're trying to reach.

- How big is the market for your product or service?
- How often do your customers use this product or service?
- What would they need to know about your product to make better and more frequent use of it?
- Where and how do your customers encounter your product, and how do they prefer to buy it?

LET YOUR FINGERS DO THE RESEARCH

If you find you don't have these answers about your target market, use the many resources at your fingertips to find the information you need.

Professional associations often make significant amounts of research and statistics available to their members. Find the association to which your customers belong—with the understanding that there may be several that reach your target audience—and garner whatever information it may provide. If your resources are slim, check the association's website to see if there are white papers or other data sources available for free.

ACCESS "BIG DATA"

The U.S. Bureau of Labor Statistics (www.bls.gov) often has information about the number of people in different age groups, professions, and income brackets. Other government sources include the U.S. Census Bureau (www.census.gov) and the Population Studies Center at the University of Michigan (www.psc.isr.umich.edu).

LOOK AT YOUR CURRENT CUSTOMERS

You may already have lots of data about your customers' locations, ages, buying habits, and more, especially if you are selling products online. Take a look at this data and see what it tells you about your current customer base. Are they residents of large cities, rural areas, or suburban communities? Are they concentrated in specific geographic locations? Do they buy your products repeatedly? What websites do they use to buy your products?

This first look gives you a starting point. Once you get there, it may be time to ask your customers for information more directly.

TAKE A SURVEY

Send all of your current customers a simple survey with a demographic element. Ask a few basic questions about their preferences, likes, and dislikes. You can use this to get their points of view about your current products and customer service, or to gauge their interest in features or services you might offer in the future.

GATHER DEMOGRAPHICS

At the end of the survey, be sure to ask for the following:

- Age range (30–39, 40–49, 50–59, etc.)
- Income range ($10,000–$20,000, $20,000–$35,000, etc.)
- Ethnicity (Caucasian, African-American, Hispanic or Latino, Asian, etc.)
- Employment status (employed full-time, self-employed, employed part-time, looking for work, homemaker, student, military, retired)
- Household composition (single, married or domestic partnership, widowed, divorced, separated)

Not all survey respondents will answer these questions, but most of them will. Their answers will tell you a great deal about your customers.

BUILD AN AVATAR

Like the avatar you might create for an online interactive game, this is a picture of your ideal customer. What do they wear? What gender are they, and is gender even important for your purposes? What is their age, and what might they look like? What do they carry to work every day? What do they do outside of work? Where do they live, and in what kind of environment? Creating this characterization can bring up points you may not have considered about the way your customer lives, works, and thinks. You don't need to create a fully functional, computer-generated model—a drawing (or even a written description) on your office whiteboard will help just as much.

Who Should Your Customer Be?

DEFINE YOUR TARGET AUDIENCE

Regardless of who your current customers are, determine who the best customers *should be* for your products or services. You'll need to look beyond your customer base to decide what kinds of customers you want.

This will be a fairly straightforward process for technical or industrial products, but if you're selling a consumer product to the general public, you may need to think carefully about the people who will first see the need for your product.

Answer some basic questions about your target customer:

- What is his age?
- Is he married? With or without children?
- Where does he live?
- What is his income level?
- What is his level of education?
- Is he a business owner? What kind of business does he own?
- What kind of job does he have? Does it matter what position he has in the organization?

GET CLUES FROM PAST CLIENTS

Take a good look at the customers who have been the most beneficial to your bottom line. What qualities make them so right for you? Chances are you will find an overlap between your most profitable clients and those who have been with you the longest.

Make a list of these qualities. If you are selling a service or product to other businesses, your best clients may all be of similar size, with a similar number of employees. They may all be in a specific industry or group of industries. For example, you may find that your best clients are law and accounting firms, or water utilities at midsize municipalities.

If you are selling to consumers, you may find that your best customers are working women, or young adults aged 18 to 30, or older adults with discretionary income.

Once you have this information, you can use it to target your audience more effectively.

GET PAST THE PURCHASING DEPARTMENT

If you sell a product to businesses, your sales team may deal with a purchasing department looking for the low bid, even if that department does not make the final buying decision. Someone within the company determines which parts, equipment, or services the company needs to achieve its objectives. It's up to you to find that decision-maker and present your customer service as a key benefit to buying your products.

WHAT PROBLEM ARE YOU SOLVING?

Whether you offer a product or a service, your offering must fill a need of some kind for your customer. Perhaps she has a problem that your product solves. The clearer you are about exactly how your product solves this problem, the better you will be at communicating this in a distinctive way to her.

If your product does not solve a problem, what is its purpose in the customer's life? Perhaps you are selling luxury items that fulfill a desire rather than a need. There's nothing wrong with selling a product with intangible benefits, but you and your staff members need to be clear on what these benefits are.

FIND THE DECISION-MAKER

The person who truly makes the buying decision may not be the customer who actually buys your product. If you sell cars, for example, you probably are aware that the person who will drive the car may not be the key decision-maker in the buying process. There may be parents (if the driver is young), adult children (if the driver is elderly), spouses, and other family members involved in deciding which car to buy. Your approach to sales must take all of these people into consideration, and your customer service package may need to reach beyond the primary driver to others.

REMEMBER THE 80/20 RULE

It's more than an old business adage—it's actually a fact that 80 percent of your business will come from 20 percent of your customers. If you can understand the service needs of that top 20 percent, you will maintain a customer base that will ensure steady income for the long term.

It won't take more than a few seconds to determine which of your customers are providing the 80 percent share of your business. Chances are you're using accounting software, so pull up a sales report for the past 12 months and see which of your clients provided the highest receivables.

WHAT MAKES A "BEST CUSTOMER"?

Take a look at your history with your best customers. What makes them the best people and companies to do business with?

They probably all share certain traits:

- **High value over a lifetime.** They regularly spend a lot of money with you.

- **Longevity.** They have probably been with you for a long time, perhaps even since you opened your business.

- **High-value purchases.** They probably buy your most expensive services or products, boosting their value with even a single purchase.

- **High profitability.** Over time, they provide the greatest profit.

If you have customers who fit all of these criteria, it's time to think about the kind of service you provide to them, and whether you can provide that same level of attention to more customers who have the potential to be as profitable for you.

APPLY THE R-F-M RULE

- **Recent:** Which customers bought goods or services from you most recently?
- **Frequent:** Which customers buy from you most often?
- **Money:** Which customers spend the most money with your company?

Look at which customers fall into at least two of these three categories, and you've got your top 20 percent. Put the greatest share of your time and energy into servicing them.

WHAT DO YOUR CUSTOMERS WANT?

Now that you have a clear understanding of your best customers, it's time to gain an equally clear picture of what they want and how you can provide it.

For example, you may be marketing a wonderful new technology that can revolutionize the way water is distributed to homes. You see all kinds of opportunities, because every community in the world needs water. Your potential customers, however, see that they will need to spend millions of dollars to install your system—and that's money they'll have to get from local or state governments through a long process that may include several election cycles. They see the value of what you're selling, but they have no way to buy it.

These same customers, however, may need a better solution for finding leaks in the water system before they become disasters. Some part of your total system may do exactly that. If you can sell that piece separately, you can get a foot in the door by solving a problem the customer is facing today.

Listen, watch, and find the way to give clients exactly what they want—and then grow the business by providing the best possible service.

How to Attract Customers

IF YOU BUILD IT . . . YOU STILL HAVE TO MARKET IT

Putting up a website and waiting for people to come to you has never been a viable strategy for business growth. Now that you know what kinds of customers you want to target, you need to start making contact with prospects. Many owners of small businesses—especially start-ups—make the mistake of believing they are too busy managing the company to go out and rustle up some business. Nothing could be further from the truth! You are your best salesperson, and you have the passion that will make people want to hear what you have to say.

ATTEND TRADE SHOWS

Go to trade shows in your market niche. Before the show, check out the list of exhibitors and attendees posted on the show's website. Who among these companies may be right for your products or services? Make a list, walk the show floor, and seek them out.

If you have the money and staff, have your own booth. There should be lots of foot traffic, so have your friendliest staff members stand out in front and talk to people as they walk by. The more engaged you and your staff are in attracting people to your booth, the more opportunities you will have to tell prospects your story.

FIND AFFINITY GROUPS

Whether it's a professional association chapter in your area or a nationwide network of club members, there's a group somewhere that will have an interest in your product. Use the web to find these people and determine the best way to reach out to them. Can you speak at one of their events? Write an informative article for the association's website? Buy banner ads on the site's landing page? When you reach the right audience with the right message, inquiries will start pouring in.

SPONSOR APPROPRIATE EVENTS

You may not have the resources to sponsor championship golf or a music-and-film festival—and these events may not be important to your target audience anyway—but you may be able to gain some visibility as a sponsor of local events attended by people in your target demographic.

If you want to reach women over 30 with discretionary income, for example, you might choose to sponsor a women's business event or a health fair. If you are targeting college students, then a summer music festival might be a good bet. For families with children, try the state fair—and show up with plenty of products to sell and samples to distribute to thousands of passers-by.

Many events offer multiple sponsorships, so you need not shoulder the entire cost to have your company associated with the event. Typically, different levels of support offer different types of exposure, so make sure you understand what you're getting.

WORK THE WEB

If you're selling a business-to-business product and you're looking for people with specific job titles within your target organizations, it's easier than ever to find them. Search a company name on LinkedIn, and up will pop a list of anyone who counts that company among their current or former employers. The next step is a little trickier: Getting in touch with these people may require you to purchase a premium membership, so you can send a private message to a person you don't know.

Alternatively, now that you have a name to match the job title, look up the person on Google to see if you can get an e-mail address, phone number, or some other way of making contact. Don't forget to try the business's website, often the most direct route to finding this kind of information.

BUILD A REPUTATION FOR QUALITY

Just as social media can turn a once-reputable company into a gaping wound in a matter of days, it can also build the positive reputation of a new company looking for visibility.

The White House Office of Consumer Affairs says that customers who get their issues resolved by customer service reps tell four to six people about it. If you make a customer happy through your excellent service, he is likely to share his experience—perhaps on Facebook, in a blog post, on Twitter, or with a photo and caption on Pinterest. If your customers are businesspeople, they may talk about you on a forum for those in their profession, or share information more casually with colleagues or clients. It all helps. When people tell good stories about you, you build the word-of-mouth (or keyboard) you need to attract more customers.

ASK FOR REFERRALS

Who better to recommend your business than your happy customers? They may not take the initiative to do so, however, unless you ask them—or, better yet, ask them to give you the names of others who may be able to use your products or services. When you have a name and contact information, you have the power to move ahead, instead of waiting for your customer to remember to bring up the subject with his friend or colleague.

Referrals from happy customers are one of the easiest ways to get new business—and one of the most overlooked by small business owners. Make asking for referrals part of your standard procedure at the end of a successful sale or project.

How to Outdo the Competition

SERVE AN UNMET NEED

Somewhere in your target industry, there's a need that isn't being met. It may not require a new technology or a breakthrough invention to meet it; it may be as simple as a spoon with a slightly different shape than the norm, or a nail that penetrates plastic without cracking it. The fact that you can see this void means you may have the insight to fill it. If your company can offer something that closes the gap in your market, you are well on your way to beating the competition and taking some of their business.

DISTINGUISH YOURSELF

Even if your product resembles something that's already on the market, you can add some features that provide important benefits—or perceived benefits. Think about Starbucks, for example. The company did not invent coffee, but it did create a coffee-drinking experience that makes people want to spend $5 for a cup of java mixed with flavorings and steamed milk. What can you offer, along with your basic product, to make it different from all the others? When you find that appeal factor, you're ready to compete.

PUT CUSTOMERS FIRST

One of the most important benefits any company can offer its customers is the feeling that their satisfaction is its top priority. This is where you cross over from selling a high-quality product to selling a whole product, as discussed in Part One. When you are willing to do whatever it takes to make your customer happy, your business grows.

MAKE CUSTOMER SATISFACTION YOUR CULTURE

It's not enough to talk the talk about customers coming first. Build a culture within your organization that makes their satisfaction a top priority. Empower your employees to offer them things like replacement products, coupons and discounts, repairs, technology training, and other benefits. This will show your customers that you stand behind your products and services, and that you won't be satisfied until they are.

RESPECT YOUR CUSTOMERS

Being friendly and helpful to customers seems obvious, but we have all had experiences with rude employees in a restaurant, pharmacy, or shop (or perhaps when we were trying to cancel our cable service). Treating customers with respect, solving their problems with grace, and thanking them for their business should be at the foundation of every company's customer service policy. Make these simple acts part of your company's culture.

COMPETE ON SERVICE, NOT PRICE

Maybe you've been to a Presidents Day mattress sale, where a hard-sell salesperson tries to beat every competitor's price. As a customer, how did you feel about that experience? Equally important, did you buy from the lowest-price company? It's more likely you chose the company that made you feel the most comfortable . Price is not the most important differentiator, especially when competing products are of similar quality. Rather than dropping your prices to unsustainable levels, offer your customers all the other things they want: on-time delivery, 30-day trial periods, longer warranties, on-site repairs, and responsive, dependable service.

KEEP YOUR PROMISES

Let's say a customer calls because a product he bought from you has broken. He would like a replacement product, and you say you will send it out that day, along with packaging, so that he can send back the broken one. Your next step should be easy: Send everything out immediately. You did what you said you would do, and this simple act of follow-through cements your relationship with the customer. If he has to remind you that he's waiting to hear from you, you lose whatever goodwill you gained by offering the replacement. When you build your customer's trust in your services, you also build repeat business.

The Best Business Attitudes

EVERY EMPLOYEE IS IN CUSTOMER SERVICE

Many businesses base their corporate culture on making sales goals, and let customer service slide down the priority list. This tells customers that you care about getting their money, but not about their value to you in the long run.

Your business may have a customer service department. On the one hand, this means someone is ready to take on whatever issues customers may have. On the other hand, it can make the rest of the staff feel that service is someone else's responsibility—something they themselves don't need to address.

The most successful businesses understand that *everyone on the staff is in customer service*. Everyone in your company must be ready to greet customers with courtesy and respect, hear their views about your products or services, solve their problems, offer them additional benefits, and deal with them honestly. Make customer service the foundation of your business, and you will attract and keep more patrons.

NOTHING SELLS LIKE ETHICS

How you deal with all your business contacts—suppliers, vendors, service providers and competitors, as well as your employees and customers—tells the world a great deal about your honesty and integrity. If you string your vendors along and don't pay them on time, if you're always looking for an angle to get more from your suppliers for less, if you talk trash about your competitors in public, you're going to develop a reputation as a business to avoid. Treat your partners in the community with respect, and your customers will hear about you and the ethical business you run. Treat them dishonestly, however, and you can bet your customers will pull away from you and look for more principled suppliers.

EMPOWER EMPLOYEES TO SAY, "OF COURSE WE CAN!"

Addressing problems with courtesy and honesty is a great starting point for your organization. You can take this a step further, however, and try to solve whatever problems may arise.

Give your employees the ability to tell customers, "Yes, of course we can fix that." Every employee who has contact with customers needs to know what tools she can use to bring their issues to a successful close. (See Part Three for ideas on what these tools might be.)

This can-do attitude gives your customers an instant feeling of relief: They know their problem will soon be solved by people who stand behind your products or services and have the power to make things right.

THE BASICS STILL APPLY

While a great deal of business today is done online, the rules of customer service have not changed dramatically. Customers still want personal service, quick response, and ease of contact with a decision-maker who can solve their problem and bring it to a close.

Make it possible for them to resolve their issue in one call or one contact with your company. If they have to make repeated phone calls, spend precious time on hold, or wait for a call or e-mail back from a representative, they will become frustrated enough to start looking for another supplier—even if you do eventually resolve the issue to their satisfaction.

KEEP IT SIMPLE

Chances are you have a mobile phone, so you have a service contract with a telecommunications supplier. If you have never read that contract, find it and take a look at the language it is written in. In most cases, even beyond the legalese, the information about your service plan has been deliberately written to be complex. What have you bought, and what kind of commitment did you sign up for? It's hard to tell. This is why just about everyone hates their mobile service provider—and why wireless carriers have some of the lowest customer service ratings of any industry.

Make it a company goal to keep language simple when you're dealing with any customer situation. If you are great at communication, you will not only find it easier to resolve issues, but you will stand out from the competition as the company which deals with the public in clear, simple terms.

How to Treat Potential Customers

THE ALL-IMPORTANT FIRST IMPRESSION

When a potential customer contacts you, or when you meet with a prospect to introduce yourself and your services, you have an opportunity to immediately begin building your reputation with her. Everything you do will leave a lasting impression, and it's up to you to ensure it's a good one.

You will talk about your product, yes, but remember that the product also includes your excellent customer service. Make sure you provide information on this in your presentation and your leave-behind package, if you have one. The more your potential customer knows about your entire offering, the more likely it is that she will choose your company over others.

MAKE YOUR PROSPECT FEEL IMPORTANT

This should be easy, because every prospect is important. Greet him warmly, and check first to see if he has time to talk to you. If this is your first contact, have a conversation with him before getting into your sales pitch. This will sharpen your eventual presentation as you tailor it to him, and also show him that you're a problem-solver looking to provide him with real value. Best of all, it will make him feel that you care about what he has to say.

FOLLOW UP WITH PROSPECTS

It's easy to let a prospect slip from your mind after your initial contact, but following up with her will demonstrate your focus on customers and commitment to service. It will also reinforce her initial impression, keeping your company and products fresh in her mind.

All of this being said, if the prospect expresses real disinterest in your company and products, put her aside for a while. Perhaps she chose another company. If so, there's no guarantee that they'll provide the high level of quality and service that you will. Be patient and follow up again in a few months.

RESPOND TO PROSPECTS

You can demonstrate your responsiveness by returning a prospect's calls and e-mails promptly, quickly furnishing her with any information she requests, and making her feel that you have made her a priority. This tells her a lot about what you will be like as a supplier, should she choose to move forward with your company and products.

CAPTURE PROSPECT INFORMATION

Make a point of taking notes during your meeting or phone conversation with your prospect. File these notes along with his contact information and any other materials or data you may have on him and his company, so you can retrieve it all quickly the next time you talk to him. With this intelligence close at hand, you can extend the conversation by following up on key points that came up during your last encounter.

PROVIDE INFORMATION YOUR PROSPECT CAN USE

Keep an eye out for information that may interest your prospect. Surprise him by sending an occasional note with a link to an article he may find useful. This tells him that you're thinking about him even though he's not paying you to do so, that you understand what he needs, and that you listened during previous conversations and took what he said to heart.

This information should *not* be about your company and its products. Instead, it may bring up a personal interest your prospect mentioned earlier, or address a problem he's trying to solve at work. Keep an ear open for the things that are important to him.

KEEP IN TOUCH

From a sales standpoint, you have a better opportunity to convert a prospect into a customer if you are diligent about following up and keeping in touch. This practice also indicates your commitment to customer service. When you call your prospect every few months to keep in touch, you can begin to form a relationship through which you will have opportunities to offer advice, tell her about new developments and features in your product line, and ask some questions about her experience with her current products or services. This demonstrates your knowledge of what you're selling—which helps build the prospect's confidence in you and your entire organization.

How to Choose
Your Words Wisely

LISTEN TO YOUR MOTHER

Do what your mother has been telling you to do since you learned to talk: Greet your customer politely, just as you would any other adult in a business setting. You will never go wrong with "Hello," "It's nice to meet you," and "Is this a good time for us to talk?" At the end of the conversation, always say "Thank you" before you close with a polite "Good-bye." This may seem obvious, but we have all had conversations with customer service representatives who did not bother with the basics of polite adult discourse.

SKIP THE SLANG

You may talk to people from all over the world and from all age groups, so your customer may not understand the slang used on the street where you live. Stick to common speech used among working adults—at least, until the person with whom you're speaking makes it clear he understands what you mean. (At this point, it might even be a good idea to use slang to help build rapport. Just keep it clean, bro.)

USE SIMPLE LANGUAGE

If you work in a technical field, you may be tempted to use all the jargon you know when talking to customers. Some of them will understand you perfectly, but others won't get a word of it—and may become frustrated with you or feel stupid when they can't follow what you're saying.

It's always better to go with plain, simple language until you know your customers well enough to gauge their comfort with the jargon of your trade. If you're troubleshooting equipment by phone, you may need to use more complex language—but you can explain the terms as you go, to help them follow your instructions carefully.

WELCOME SUGGESTIONS

If a customer e-mails you with a product improvement he'd like to see, thank him for the suggestion even if it's ridiculous. It's always better to respond with, "That's a really interesting idea! I'll pass it on to the product development team," than with, "This product will never do that," or, "We won't be going in that direction." The fact that he offered you the suggestion means he's excited about your product, at least enough to think about what he'd like to do differently with it. Meet that enthusiasm with an equivalent amount of welcome and thanks.

APOLOGIZE

When a customer calls or e-mails with a problem, it's taken time out of his day to do so. The problem with your product may have caused him to lose data, or he may be unable to finish a time-sensitive task. Whatever the issue, he needs to know that you and your company care about his inconvenience.

Apologize even if it was the customer's fault. Say, "I'm so sorry that happened. Let's see what we can do to fix this as quickly as possible."

It's appropriate to take this a step further, saying, "I can understand how frustrating that must be," or, if more casual language seems right, "Wow, that's really frustrating!" However you say it, a simple apology can defuse a lot of anger and frustration. It starts the conversation off with the customer getting a sense that you truly understand him and want to help.

BE GENUINE

What you say is important, but how you say it can be equally key. No one wants to talk to a corporate drone reading from a canned script in a remote call center—not because these workers are bad people, but because they sound like they're saying what they've been told to say, instead of having a real conversation. Even if you're in a call center, you can address callers in the same way you would a friend or coworker. Treat them the way you would want to be treated if you were on the other end of the line.

FINISH WITH A QUESTION

Suppose you're responding to a question from a customer about how to use a particular product feature. You write her an e-mail to answer the question, but there's a chance she won't fully understand the response, or that the solution you've provided solves the wrong problem.

You can leave the door open for her to come back to you with additional questions. All you have to do is finish the e-mail with your own question: "Did this answer solve your problem?"

Chances are very good that your customer will come back with a note of thanks, or that she will reply to your e-mail with an additional question. Either way, you've prolonged the conversation, a key element in building a relationship with her—and in making sure her problem did indeed get solved.

You can also finish your e-mail with, "Is there any other way I can help today?" This sounds like a pleasantry, but if the customer has another issue, it gives her the opening to bring it up.

Inbound Call Greetings

KEEP IT BRIEF

A recorded message is the first thing callers hear when they try to reach your customer service department. You can make the experience less tedious for them by creating a friendly, efficient series of messages and prompts to move them quickly through the system.

Start with a welcoming message that lets them know this is a professional organization and that you want to help them resolve their issue. Keep the greeting short: The faster they get to the customer service representative, the happier they will be.

USE CONSISTENT LANGUAGE

See if this experience sounds familiar: You call a customer help line with your latest statement in hand. The prompts in the automated system ask you to key in your customer ID number. You look at your statement, and you cannot find it. There's an account number, a group number, and a policy number, but nothing labeled as a customer ID. What do you do now?

You can save your customers a great deal of stress and confusion by making sure your terminology is the same on your statements, your product literature, your website, and your incoming message recording. Double-check all of your communication pieces before your recording goes live.

EDIT YOUR SCRIPT

Here are some ways to keep the greeting and prompts on your automated message center as brief as possible.

- **Start with a greeting.** "Thank you for calling ABC Company."

- **Resist the urge to advertise.** An advertising message after the greeting is just an irritant. She has already called your company; chances are she knows what you do.

- **Eliminate repetition.** There's no need to say "please" before every prompt.

- **Assume your caller has done this before.** Instead of, "If you know the extension of the person you wish to reach, you may enter it at any time," use a shortened version: "Enter your party's extension at any time." Then move on to the list of more generic prompts.

- **Say the department name, then the number.** "For Sales, press 1. For Service, press 2, and so on. If you say the number before the name, the listener will wait for the name to see if she needs to remember the number, and may end up forgetting the latter.

PROVIDE A ROUTE TO A REAL PERSON

While many customers can find the help they need among the prompts on your automated system, some have complex issues or technical questions that need the help of a human being. You can help these customers access their preferred help method by providing a way to reach a representative in the first or second menu. This will reduce frustration for those who already know, when they pick up the phone, that they'll need more help than the recorded system can provide.

How to Address a Customer

BE RESPECTFUL

It goes without saying (although we're saying it anyway) that every customer must be treated with respect. This involves looking him in the eye, listening when he speaks, allowing him to finish his statement, and acknowledging that what he says has value. Rolling your eyes, laughing at what he has requested, scoffing and making sarcastic statements like, "Yeah, that's gonna happen," and otherwise disparaging him, will never help you provide good service.

USE A PERSON'S NAME

It may be common in your culture to call someone "dude," "mate," or "girl," but these are terms for people with whom you have close relationships. Your customers should always be addressed by name. Make it a rule to address them as Mr. or Ms. at first, unless they instruct you otherwise (e.g., "Please call me Jane"). In-between use of their names, it's appropriate to call customers "sir" or "miss." It's also appropriate to say, for example, "May I call you Jane?" In the rare case that the customer says no, smile and keep calling them Ms. Smith.

ALWAYS USE THE CUSTOMER'S EARNED TITLE

If your customer has a title—Doctor, Reverend, Professor, Lord, Sir, or Dame—be sure to use it in speaking with them. This not only shows respect for their achievement, but it also proves that you are paying attention to detail.

EASY ON THE MA'AM

When to use "ma'am" or "miss"? Many women over age 30 feel that "ma'am" implies that they are middle-aged or older. You may notice that in Starbucks franchises, the word "ma'am" is rarely used by the baristas. All women are called "miss"—a deliberate choice to avoid offense. Most women leave the counter smiling, so this simple technique clearly works.

GENDER GUESSWORK

If your contact with customers is mostly by phone, you may not always be able to tell from their name and voice whether they are male or female. If you don't know, ask. There's nothing wrong with saying, "Our records say Mister Terry Jones. Is this correct?" Clearing up the confusion at the beginning of the call can make a positive difference in customers' overall impression of your service.

DON'T BE LIKE COMCAST

In January 2015, a customer of Comcast in Spokane, Washington, was stunned at the way his last bill was addressed after he cancelled his cable service because of financial hardship. The Comcast employee who had taken the cancellation had changed Ricardo Brown's name to read, "Asshole Brown."

Comcast scrambled to apologize, refunding two years of the customer's bills and firing the employee responsible. This incident, however, will live on as a textbook case of what a customer service representative should not do—at least, not if he wants to keep his job.

What Tone to Use

WHEN TO PICK UP A CALL

If you're working in a call center or you're the main customer service representative for a small company, chances are you spend a lot of time on the phone. Call center managers around the world recommend that you pick up during the third ring. This is not so quick and abrupt that it startles the caller, and not so long that he gets impatient before you answer.

HOW TO ANSWER

Many call centers and other customer service lines are fond of adding a long slogan statement to the customer service rep's script when they first answer the phone. If the caller has been waiting in a queue for some time, however, she will find this infuriating. Make your greeting short and simple.

- **Wrong:** "Smith's Technical Support, Home of the Two-Way, 24-Hour Mega-Response Action Team. This is Fred speaking, how may I help you?"
- **Right:** "Hi, this is Fred, how may I help you?"

SMILE WHEN YOU ANSWER

It's an old trick, but it works: Smile as you pick up the phone. The smile takes hold and changes your voice, making it sound as if you're happy to be at work and can't wait to help your customer with her issue. You may even find that it sincerely makes you pleased to be there.

FIND YOUR NATURAL GREETING

Some people are comfortable answering the phone with, "Good morning," or "Good day," while others sound stiff and unnatural. Strive for a conversational greeting that feels right for you, as long as it's in acceptable business language. ("Wassup," for example, would not be appropriate.)

GO BEYOND THE SCRIPT

If a customer wanted an automated response, she would have found her answers online. She called your company because she wants to talk to a real, thinking person who can listen to all the things that make her issue unique, and help her find a lasting solution.

Perhaps you have a customer support software program that generates answers to common questions for your service representatives. This approach has been proven to work, and will resolve many issues. But your reps also need to be able to listen to the customer, have a real conversation with her, and talk her through the solution that's right for her. Give them the freedom to speak naturally and conversationally, and to try answers that may not be scripted.

TO MATCH OR NOT TO MATCH?

If your customer service interactions are usually in person, it can be tempting to match your client's tone and speaking style. For example, if he is particularly casual and uses a lot of slang, you may want to do the same when you talk with him. If you go down this path, however, your relationship can become equally loose and casual—so when you have to discuss a sticky business situation, a price increase, or the terms of a contract, you may have difficulty regaining a businesslike tone and relationship.

You don't need to remain completely formal, but maintaining businesslike language will help you set the tone for your whole interaction with the customer. This is especially true if you communicate with him mostly by e-mail, because the lack of vocal nuance can make a perfectly innocent sentence seem like a raging argument.

THREE PARTS TO COMMUNICATION

Researcher Albert Mehrabian discovered in 1967 that communication is made of up three unequal parts:

1. The words themselves make up 7 percent.
2. The tone you use when speaking makes up 38 percent.
3. Your body language when you speak makes up 55 percent.

If you correspond by phone or e-mail, you lose the body language—so your tone needs to work harder for you. This is one of the reasons emoticon symbols have become so popular: They help convey the intended tone that may not come across in the words of an e-mail or text. It's up to you and your employer to decide whether you wish to use these symbols in your correspondence with customers; if you do choose to use them, choose ones that are generic enough for anyone to understand.

YOU ARE NOT A ROBOT, SO DON'T SOUND LIKE ONE

No one wants to talk with someone who can only read from a prepared script, but many new customer service reps are more comfortable sticking with the language on the screen. You can avoid this robotic approach with a little rehearsal time.

- **Become familiar with the language of your job.** If you're working with technology that is new to you, you'll find that your comfort level grows exponentially if you take the time to learn how it works. Your customers will hear confidence in your voice or e-mails, and you'll have better responses and interactions with them.

- **Rehearse the phrases you use most,** and find a way to say them naturally and in your own words. Chances are you would rarely say in real life, "I sincerely apologize for the inconvenience this has caused." You might actually say, "Wow, I hope this hasn't caused a major problem! Let me help you make this right."

EMPATHY IS KING

Put yourself in your customer's place. It's 4:30 p.m., she has a presentation due the next day, and suddenly the fabulous animation software you sell has frozen solid. She's under the gun, and no one can help her but you. Can you identify with her stress and desperation? That's empathy. When you can ease your customers' pain and express your understanding of their situation, they will feel like you are a willing, dependable partner eager to help them get things back on track.

How to Think About Customer Service

FIRST, THINK ABOUT THE EXPERIENCE

When we think about customer service, we can't help but turn to Apple's late CEO, Steve Jobs, to learn from the very best. Jobs's often-articulated approach was: "You've got to start with the customer experience and work back toward the technology—not the other way around."

As great as Apple products are per se, Jobs believed the customer service experience was absolutely integral to them. Thus, for instance, his company came up with the Genius Bar—a place that any product user can go to for free, in-person technical assistance from a well-trained expert—by modeling the approach used by Ritz-Carlton hotels with their highly-regarded concierge service. By bringing the customer service model up to a whole new level, Apple carved out a niche and soon came to dominate the global wireless technology market.

What can your company do to break away from the pack? It's worth thinking differently to find out.

YOUR CUSTOMERS ARE
YOUR BEST FRIENDS

How do you treat your closest friends? Chances are you value their time and look forward to your next interaction with them. You give them priority in your life, making room for them and listening to everything that's good and bad in their lives. When they have a problem, you move heaven and earth to help them.

Your customers deserve the same kind of treatment. They spend money with your company, and so support your entire way of life—they pay your salary, fund your vacations, and put your children through college. In return, they need attention when they run into difficulty with your products, or when they need rush services on short notice.

It's up to you and your company to deliver on the promise of this relationship by making your customer service accessible, easy, pleasant, and effective. When you do this, you build loyal relationships with your clients—and they tell their friends and business associates about your fine service. Everyone wins!

CUSTOMERS WILL SPEND MORE
FOR BETTER SERVICE

A survey by American Express in 2011 produced a critically important finding: Seven in 10 Americans said they were willing to spend more with companies they believed provided excellent customer service.

This means great service is a selling point—and a benefit that could have a direct effect on your bottom line. In fact, building a strong customer service element within your company can increase your bottom line, even if it increases the price of your products. A reputation for fine service will help you attract customers who value this kind of relationship.

BE GRATEFUL FOR EVERY COMPLAINING CUSTOMER

The White House Office of Consumer Affairs tells us that for every customer who complains to a company about its products or services, 26 others don't bother to do so. Of those, 91 percent never buy from that company again. Customers who bring you their product problems give you the rare opportunity to fix them—and, equally important, to make them feel good about their experience with you. This allows you to build a potentially long-lasting relationship with them, instead of losing them in a sea of quietly grumbling others whom you'll never reach.

GREAT SERVICE IS WHAT YOUR CUSTOMER THINKS IT IS

Twentieth-century songwriter Fats Waller once wrote a lyric that you may recognize from the Broadway musical *Ain't Misbehavin'*: "Find out what they like and how they like it, and let 'em have it just that way."

Waller was writing about amorous lovers, but the concept has value for customer service as well. A survey by Lee Resources discovered that while 80 percent of companies say they deliver "superior" customer service, only 8 percent of their customers think they *actually* do. The disconnect here is shocking, and it reveals something very important: What you think is a wonderful service offering may not be what the customer wants.

Ask your clients about your service. Find out if you're missing the boat. Are they getting what they need from your company? If not, what do they need that you do not yet provide? This may open some doors to product innovation, but it should also tell you a lot about how effective your customer service operation actually is.

TRAIN EMPLOYEES TO BE EXPERTS

As we said earlier, every employee is in customer service. This means that anyone in your company who interacts with customers must have a working knowledge of your products and services—especially if you're selling technology. You will always have technical experts on staff who can respond to the most difficult cases, but your customers will likely talk to other people in your company—the CEO, a sales rep, support staff, or your dedicated customer service team—before they reach the technology professional.

No matter who picks up the phone to talk with a customer, they need to know what your products are, what they do, how they work, what benefits they provide, and what kinds of things most often go wrong with them. This knowledge will help customers resolve their issues faster.

MAKE IT EASY

Have you ever called the Internal Revenue Service? If not, thank your lucky stars. Possibly the world's most dysfunctional organization as far as customer service goes, the IRS has numerous, far-ranging, overly segmented and specialized call centers, all bogged down with as long as one-hour wait times to speak to a human representative. Most of the time, that rep will tell you that you need to call a different number for the specific service you need—which means another hour on hold while you try to reach someone who may once again be unable to help you.

The keys to excellent service are simplicity, responsiveness, and the ability to get a problem resolved in one phone call or e-mail. Strive for this level of customer service, and you will trample your competition.

PART

GENERAL RULES

ow that some basics are in place, we can delve more deeply into the anatomy of your interaction with customers.

Every time you come into contact with clients or prospects, you have an opportunity to demonstrate your commitment to customer service. Your customer may order products from you and expect to receive the order on time, with all of the correct items in the box. He may need some additional help with documents such as statements or reports, or with custom features that you offer at premium prices. If you are a service business, such as a law firm or accounting firm, he may need a great deal of your time to accomplish a specific goal. Each time you get one of these requests, you have an opportunity to provide him with great service—and when you deliver on this promise, you build his trust and pave the way for repeat business.

Equally important, you need to be ready and willing to deal with your customers' problems as they arise. No matter how dependable your products are, or how brilliantly you provide professional services, sometimes things will go wrong. The way you recover from this will tell your customers all they need to know about your company. Whether they pick up the phone and call you, contact you by e-mail, or chat with you online, they expect their issue to be resolved; they want answers and a quick resolution in as few steps as possible. In this part, we'll talk about ways to make every customer service call as effective and painless as possible.

Converting a Prospect Into a Customer

STAND OUT

Give potential clients a good reason to choose you—a feature no one else offers, a solution to a specific problem, or a reputation for the finest customer service in your niche.

LET THE SALES PITCH FIT YOUR PRODUCT OR SERVICE

When you see commercials for personal injury law firms, what do you think? The first thing that goes through many people's minds is, "Respectable law firms don't advertise." Let your sales methods reflect the quality of your product or service. There's no need to stoop to mass-market tactics, hard sell, or other sales tricks to bring in business. Maintain your high standards for your message and your company's image.

LET THE WEB WORK FOR YOU

When prospects first begin searching for the right supplier, they may not understand what their needs actually are. You can help them zero in on these needs by providing informative content on your website. White papers, reports, news articles, and blogs written by your in-house experts can help differentiate you from your competition.

ASK QUESTIONS

The more you know about your prospect's needs, the better you can address the things she cares about most. Ask about the kinds of challenges she faces, and respond with the ways your product or service can solve them. If your product does not address her concerns, move on to your next prospect. Your time is valuable, so don't fall into the trap of trying to close every single potential client—especially if she's not the right fit for you.

CONSIDER YOUR PROSPECTS' ROI

If you can legitimately offer your prospect a return on investment (ROI) when he uses your product, say so. Everyone wants to save money—and cost savings from using your product or service can be just the incentive your prospect needs to take your offer to the decision-makers, or make the buying decision himself. If you can prove that customers see a reduction in expenses by using your product, so much the better. Have PDFs of ROI graphs and charts, testimonials, and other tools ready to send out to prospects.

FOLLOW UP

Once your prospect shows some interest, make a note to follow up with her at a specific time. Check back to see if she has additional questions you can answer, if she knows the time frame for making a decision about your offer, and if there is any other information you can provide to help her in the decision-making process. This demonstration of your interest and helpfulness can tilt the scales in your direction.

Listening

MORE SURVEYS

We talked about the value of surveys in finding out who your customers are. But you can also use them to learn about what your customers need, and where your company may need to improve. Ask questions like these:

- What was your overall experience like?
- Would you use this product/service again?
- What was the purpose of your call/website visit/ e-mail inquiry?
- Was your issue resolved in one contact?
- What was the most positive part of your visit?
- What was the most negative part?
- In what ways does our company need to improve?

ASK AT THE CHECKOUT

If you have a brick-and-mortar store, or if your sales take place online or by phone, you have an opportunity to gauge your customers' experience while they are transacting business with you. Build this capability into your checkout process, whether it's a quick three-question survey that pops up after the sale, a couple of questions from your sales representative, or a friendly inquiry from the person behind the register.

CREATE ONLINE COMMUNITIES

One of the most effective ways to reach many people at once is through opt-in online forums, in which customers interact with one another. Those who visit these forums will make candid comments about their experience with your company. While some of these comments may be on the fringe—and some conversations may spiral down into less-than-useful commentary—you will find that most customers share real experiences and genuine thoughts about your company, its products, and their overall usefulness.

NO TIME LIMITS

If you have an inbound customer service function, your customer service representatives should feel comfortable having a conversation with a caller. Time limits, quotas, and other arbitrary goals can keep reps from gathering the rich information that will help you grow your business. Encourage them to ask questions about what made the customer call, why he chose your company's products over others, and what his experience has been like as a product user.

MAKE IT EASY FOR CUSTOMERS TO CONTACT YOU

Some companies bury their customer support information on their websites, but this strategy only keeps them from hearing the feedback they need to succeed. Make your support line or live chat easy to find with a prominently positioned button on your site's home page, and provide clear information about your support line's hours and the options available to customers.

THE TRUTH IS OUT THERE

Like it or not, your customers—and often your prospects—
know the truth about your company, both good and bad.
People talk to one another, especially people who are in the
same kind of business. In today's social media society, they
also post reviews to websites like Yelp and Angie's List, write
140-character messages about you on Twitter, discuss your
company's stumbles on Facebook, and so on. Get ahead of
all of this by searching these sites frequently to see what
they're saying about you.

Making It Right

RESPOND TO SOCIAL MEDIA

So you've Googled and searched Twitter and found that there are complaints out there about your company. What can you do about them?

First, respond to the complainant publicly. Post a direct response and ask her to contact you directly at your e-mail address or phone number. If she posted her own e-mail or phone number, get in touch with her directly to see if you can make it right with her. Once the issue has been resolved, ask her to repost to the forum or website with an account of your response. If she doesn't, you can post it yourself.

OWN THE MISTAKE

If a product breaks or doesn't perform properly, a delivery doesn't arrive on time, or your service goes out and inconveniences hundreds of people, it's time to take ownership of that problem. It doesn't matter to customers if your vendor let you down or a storm took out your power. You need to apologize and tell them what you will offer (credit on the next bill, free services, or a replacement product) to make it right.

DO WHAT YOU SAY YOU WILL

If you promise customers that you will get back to them in three days with a resolution to their problem, get back to them within three days. If it actually takes you two weeks to contact them with the solution, you'll lose their trust—and you might make them angrier than they were when the original issue came up. Follow through on your promise, and you'll retain your customers' confidence.

DON'T OVERPROMISE

Let's say your company has a major electrical service outage, rendering it unable to make products and deliver orders on time. You may think, "I need to tell customers they will have their products in three days." In reality, you don't have control over when power will be restored to your plant. Give customers a realistic time frame in which to expect their deliveries, so they can plan accordingly. If you say, "I want to be honest with you, I don't know when we'll have power—and I don't want to overpromise and disappoint you twice," they will appreciate your candor.

BE PROACTIVE ABOUT PROBLEMS

A product recall, a fire in a plant, a major weather event, a bad batch of parts sneaking its way into your manufacturing system—any of these can mean a sudden, even catastrophic change in the way you do business in the short term. It's critical that you contact your customers right away, letting them know they should expect a slowdown in delivery or a need to replace products they already have. Don't wait until the issue hits the news; mobilize your customer service operation and get on the phones.

OFFER ALTERNATIVES

In many cases, you can help your customers by offering them options:

- A similar product from your inventory
- A replacement for a product that is defective
- A new product in a longer-than-usual time frame
- A credit to their account
- If all else fails, a full refund

Knowing that there are choices can help ease a customer's anxiety and disappointment in a bad situation.

Apologizing

MOVE QUICKLY

As soon as you know there's a problem, start working on your apology. Once you understand the scope and magnitude of the problem for your customers, let them know what happened—and how sorry you are—as quickly as you can. If you are concerned about taking responsibility for an issue that may have formed up the supply chain from your company—for example, if you package food products and a grower sent you tainted spinach—you should still apologize for the effect this has had on your clients. Assure them that you're searching for the cause and will report back to them as soon as you manage to identify it.

SAY YOU ARE SORRY

This is not the time to use public relations jargon or wiggly words. Say it in plain language: "We are so sorry for the inconvenience this has caused, and for the impact on your life (or business)." Keep saying it until the issue is resolved to the customers' satisfaction.

GO WIDE

If the problem has affected only a segment of your customers, it's still a good idea to tell your entire customer base what's happening. Send two different e-mails, and post both of these to your blog or website—wherever you will reach the most people. In one message, explain the issue to affected customers and apologize for the effect it will have on them. In the second message, reassure those who have not been directly affected by the problem, and explain that you want to make sure everyone has accurate information on it.

TELL CUSTOMERS WHAT HAPPENED

When an issue arises, affected customers want an explanation; they want to know that you have taken the time and put in the effort to fully understand what went wrong. They want to know that you will prevent the same thing from happening again, so they can feel comfortable about their continued business with you. Give them a clear, plain-language description of the problem and the steps you have taken to resolve it. As Adam Ramshaw at the Australian strategic planning firm Genroe said, "Customers like good news, they dislike bad news, but they really hate surprises."

BE SORRY—SINCERELY

It may seem like an obvious point, but it's important to both say you're sorry and show it through your actions. We all remember the behavior of BP's CEO, Tony Hayward, after his company dumped millions of gallons of oil in the Gulf of Mexico. Hayward told reporters at a news conference that he wished he could get his life back, and then spent time entertaining guests on his yacht while Gulf residents and fishing operations struggled to maintain their livelihoods. Your issues are likely to be on a much smaller scale, but cancel your prior plans and get the problem resolved.

THEN TELL THEM WHY IT WON'T HAPPEN AGAIN

When it's all over and things are back to normal, tell customers what you did to make sure you never have this problem again. Did you overhaul your system? Fire a vendor? Find a new vendor who has special safety features in place? Implement a new procedure in-house? Whatever you did, explain it to your patrons in a way that fosters their confidence in you.

Following Up

BEGIN WITH "AFTER THE SALE"

Most companies are great about following up with customers until they make a sale, but once a product has been bought, the follow-up dries up. Put your customer service organization on the follow-up process: Call your clients to see how the product is working for them, ask for their impressions, and see if they have any questions your reps can answer. This way, not only can you stop small issues from becoming big problems, but you can also demonstrate to customers that they matter even when they're not spending money with you.

MAKE SPECIAL OFFERS

Many companies offer special promotions only to new customers, irking existing customers who are paying more yet aren't eligible. Make special offers to them as well, so as to let them know they still have value for you. This will also give your reps a reason to call them and touch base with them—and it will cement long-term customer loyalty.

FOLLOW UP ON ISSUES

Customers who call for technical assistance or problem resolution want their issues fixed in one phone call. Sometimes, however, it's hard to tell if an issue has been fixed for the long term, especially if it's related to software or the like. If this is the case, make a note to wait a day or two and call your client back; make certain he's not still struggling and madder than ever at your company. Give him the help he needs to get back on track.

KEEP TRACK OF CALLS

There are few things customers hate more than having to start over and re-explain their issue when they call customer service a second time. According to *Harvard Business Review,* 56 percent of respondents to a business satisfaction survey complained of exactly this issue. You can avoid frustrated customers by keeping thorough notes on each call, and making them available on your customer service software. This will also help you flag callers for follow-up, and make sure their problem has been solved.

JUMP ON A PROBLEM

If you are getting a number of calls from customers about a problem with a specific product, find out what's causing it—and get all of your clients on the phone or e-mail to let them know you've discovered this. If you don't have a solution yet but are working on it, tell them so and keep working. Don't wait for the problem to escalate into a crisis.

SEND A NOTE

Few things are simpler than sending an informal e-mail to customers, making sure a problem has been properly resolved. Here's a general draft.

Hi Joe,

Thanks so much for giving me the opportunity to help you out yesterday with _____. I just want to follow up and make sure things are working properly for you at this point. Would you just confirm?

If you need more assistance, I'm happy to help. Shoot me back an e-mail and I will see what needs to be done.

Thanks again,

Jack

Reassuring

BUYER'S REMORSE

After a customer has purchased a product—particularly an expensive one—she may move quickly from pleasure to regret. This may come from difficulty getting the product to do what she bought it to do, or unclear product instructions, or the simple fact that she couldn't actually afford it. You can save the sale by probing to identify the issue and correct the problem.

THE PURSUIT OF PERFECTION

Many customers expect an item to live up to an impossible standard, especially if it was expensive. Few products or services are perfect in every way, so any purchase creates the potential for some kind of disappointment. If your customer sees only the faults in your offering, reassure him by reminding him of the benefits that convinced him to buy it in the first place; do your best to refocus his attention on all the things that are right with it.

FORGOTTEN TRAINING

Business motivational speaker Tony Alessandra notes that people forget 75 percent of what they hear after two days. Even if your top-notch training team spent days teaching your customers to use your products, these customers may not retain that information. Gently remind them of things they may have forgotten since training, and stick with them until they get the product to work properly.

SHOW SINCERE CONCERN

When a customer calls with a problem, she wants to believe that you and your company care about solving it. Listen to the issue and sympathize before you launch into a solution. If you say, "Wow, that sounds really upsetting! Let's see what we can do to make this right," your customer will immediately begin to relax. Think how much more effective this response is than the standard call center response—silence, followed by reading a scripted answer from a database.

NEVER MAKE YOUR CUSTOMER FEEL FOOLISH

There's an old story about a customer who called the customer service line for one of the personal computer companies because he mistook the CD drive for a cup holder. We can laugh at this now, but no matter what a customer's issue may be, it is frustrating for him and needs to be treated as something that deserves to be solved. It may be a true technical glitch that requires a repair or replacement, or a misunderstanding of the instructions, but it has caused this customer to lose time, effort, and perhaps even business—it must be taken seriously.

FOLLOW UP BY PHONE

A phone call from you a day or two after you've helped a customer will reassure her that you're there when she needs you—and that you're serious about her satisfaction with your product.

Acknowledging

HEAR EVERYTHING

Customers sometimes contact you with a whole list of concerns, and you want to be certain you've gathered them all so you can resolve them effectively and maintain your positive relationship with the client. Listen carefully, and acknowledge each of his qualms by repeating it. Ask him, "Do you have more concerns, or have we covered them all?" When he acknowledges that you've heard everything, you're ready to start looking for solutions.

SUMMARIZE WHAT YOU HEAR

Your customers need to know that you heard and understood their problem. The best way to demonstrate this is to repeat it back after you've heard the whole story: "So what I hear you saying is, your printer worked just fine until yesterday, and now it keeps telling you that there's a paper jam, but you've opened all the doors and lifted the lid and looked inside, and there's no paper jam. Is that correct?" Once they agree, you can move on to the solution.

LISTEN ACTIVELY

Expand your acknowledgment of your customer's problem throughout the story, by repeating and summarizing along the way. "So you were printing a long document, and everything was fine, and then the printer simply jammed and won't clear, is that right?" You're not looking for solutions yet—you're just letting the customer know you've heard what she said. This validates her experience, and may also encourage her to provide additional details.

ACKNOWLEDGE ANGER

Some customers call a service line, fire off an e-mail to a customer support center, or walk up to a retail counter with the assumption that they'll play out a scene in a life script in which no one appreciates their pain. They will approach you expecting you to be just another indifferent service rep. You can take control of this transaction by acknowledging their anger at whatever issue has brought them to you ("I can see that you're angry, and I understand why"), and working through it until they're satisfied. Your empathy and positive outlook might actually turn this into a positive experience for both of you.

MAKE THE CUSTOMER VISIBLE

How often have you stood at the host's station in a restaurant and wondered why no passing staff member seemed to notice you were there? It only takes a second to say to a customer, "Hi, we'll be with you in just a moment," to let him know that you've seen him and realize he's waiting. In a retail situation, ask him, "Is someone helping you?" or, "Have you found what you need?" If no one has offered him assistance, it's your opportunity to make him feel welcome, acknowledged, and valued.

RECOGNIZE REPEAT CUSTOMERS

Some of us have restaurants we frequent, both because the food there is terrific and because the service is great. Think about the times you've arrived at your favorite place and had the staff wave or bring over your "usual" drink order without you having to ask. This kind of service makes you feel like you're part of a family—the stock-in-trade of a locally-owned neighborhood eatery. Acknowledge your repeat customers with a smile and a greeting, and you will make them feel like a valued part of your business.

Showing Empathy

SAY "I UNDERSTAND"

Empathy is about relating to what the customer is feeling. When you articulate this by saying, "I understand how frustrating that must be," your customer not only knows you're listening, but she can tell that you want to help. This alone can take some of the stress out of the situation for her.

MAKE A PERSONAL CONNECTION

Putting yourself in the customer's position can go a long way in building trust and a sense that you really understand what he's been through. Tell him, "I would also be pretty angry if that happened to me," and he may suddenly become less angry. You're making a connection that will help you work through the problem together.

EMPATHY WORDS

One of the ways to actively listen to a customer's issue is to react to the story she's telling. You may have a natural, spontaneous reaction to it, especially if it is difficult or moving —you'll find yourself saying, "Oh, wow!" or, "Oh, my goodness!" while she speaks. Even exclamations like, "No way!" can be appropriate. Keep it clean, though; you represent your company, so avoid profanity or slang with ambiguous meanings.

I'M SO SORRY

Chances are you didn't cause the problem, but you can still apologize on behalf of your company. Your customer has been inconvenienced and deserves an apology; the sooner he receives it, the sooner you can move past his frustration and begin solving his issue. Say, "I am really sorry you had that experience. Let's see what we can do to get things back on track." The customer will let go of his anger and earn the satisfaction he craves.

"THANKS SO MUCH FOR TELLING ME"

Not only has the customer come to you with an opportunity to solve a problem for her, but she has also alerted you to a situation that may not be isolated. For this, she deserves your gratitude. Whether she's letting you know that one of your products is defective, or that she recently received bad service in one of your establishments, or that she has discovered a gap in your product instructions or a bug in your software, she's bringing a potential system flaw to your attention. Once you have listened to her story and acknowledged her inconvenience, thank her for providing this information. You will make her feel that she has done right in contacting you, and that her effort is appreciated.

Explaining

BRIDGE THE PERCEPTION GAP

Remember those "magic eye" posters that became three-dimensional if you stared at them just right? Not everyone could see the raised image popping out of the poster, no matter how long they stared or how much they squinted. The same thing can happen when two different people approach a new concept. You may think an idea is obvious, but your customer may not see it at all. It's up to you to turn his perception around by teaching him how to get the most out of it—in this case, out of your product or service. Be patient, and try explaining in straightforward, jargon-free language.

KEEP IT SIMPLE

You may be required to explain something technical or complicated to a customer. Keep in mind that what seems simple to you may not be at all simple to her, especially if she's trying to learn about a new technology. Take her through the procedure or idea step by step, to see where she gets stuck along the way. Perhaps she's embarrassed to admit she doesn't understand a term you're using, so try using plain-English words instead of technical ones whenever possible.

BE GRATEFUL FOR QUESTIONS

When your customer asks questions, he's showing interest in what you have to say and actively participating in the learning process. You may wish he'd stop interrupting, but his questions tell you where he may be having trouble understanding—so be grateful for the opportunity to answer them and keep your explanation moving toward a successful conclusion. When customers don't ask for clarification and seem to give up on getting the answers they need, it can mean that they don't believe they can understand the concept at all . . . and they may lose faith in your product or service. Questions are a good indicator that you both want to achieve the same goal.

DON'T TALK DOWN

There's a delicate balance between using simple language and talking down to your customers. If you begin to feel like you're Big Bird, you're probably oversimplifying your explanation. Instead of saying, "Okay, now do you see the red thingy next to the big blinking light?" try saying, "When the light goes on, you'll see a red lever to the right of it. Push that up into the starting position." Your language is still basic, but not patronizing.

ASK QUESTIONS

You can ascertain your customer's understanding of words and concepts used with your products by asking some clarifying questions. Try, "Do you know what I mean when I say 'volatile organic chemicals?'" If the answer is yes, you can continue with your conversation. If the answer is no, however, you need to explain this term before you go any further, or your customer won't understand anything else you have to say.

ANALOGIES HELP MAKE CONCEPTS CLEARER

An analogy is a comparison between two things that can aid in explaining or clarifying something. For example, you might explain the human body's nervous system by comparing it to an old-fashioned, hardwired telephone service, something many people still have in their homes. Signals move rapidly through the system on wires until they are received at the right phone number, where the signal makes the phone ring. The same is true for the nervous system—when a finger touches something, the signal races through nerves and across synapses until it reaches the brain, which sends out the sensation of feeling. This happens just as instantaneously as making a phone call (faster, in fact).

You can use analogies like this one to help your customers understand how a technical product works, or how your services will benefit them. Using a familiar concept makes it easier to comprehend something that seems dauntingly complicated.

Limiting

CORRALLING THE CHRONIC COMPLAINER

Perhaps you have a customer who feels the need to be heard regularly. You may hear from her every few days with a complaint by phone or e-mail, or you may run into her often when she comes into your store or restaurant. She may feel she is entitled to tell you everything she's thinking every time she sees you. While many of her criticisms may be valid, this level of interaction monopolizes your time.

The next time this customer approaches you, try corralling her intentions. Offer to set up a meeting with her where she can tell you everything that's on her mind. Say, "Look, right now isn't a good time, but I want to hear what you have to say. Let me grab my calendar and we can set aside half an hour to talk." She may agree to the meeting, or she may decide it's not important enough to take up that much of her own time—either way, you've demonstrated your interest without allowing her to corner you.

THE 5 PERCENT RULE

Small business consultant Rhonda Abrams recommends listening carefully to the complaints of a demanding customer, to find the kernel of truth within the barrage of information. "You may perceive 95 percent of the complaint as inaccurate," she says, "but if you listen for the 5 percent you can agree with, [the interaction] turns into a learning opportunity." That small percentage may lead to a genuine improvement in your product, service, or support organization.

BEWARE OF SPECIAL FAVORS

Some customers believe they have a special relationship with your company, and so can demand perks that others do not receive. A client may ask you to do some work for free, lower your prices just for him, throw in extras that are not usually included in a sale, or forgive late payments without penalty. Once you capitulate, it can be very hard to backtrack to treating him like you do everyone else.

Start by establishing a schedule of offers that you can make to any customer: discounts on specific bonus items with a sale, coupons for free merchandise when a product does not perform to their expectations, or invitations to special events, to name just a few. If a client begins to feel he can demand such things without cause (say, when there's no product purchase or complaint), you can explain in the nicest possible language that you must follow company policy for such things. "If I do it for you, I have to do it for everyone, and the company guidelines just don't allow me to do that" is a perfectly valid answer.

DEFINE LIMITS FOR EMPLOYEES

Hard-and-fast rules for dealing with customers rarely allow employees to build long-lasting relationships. They need to know how far they can go to make things right with a client, even if it means bending the rules a little to make her happy. What if she brings a brand-new product back to your store and freely admits that her lack of understanding of how it works caused her to damage it? Will you offer her a new product and some training in how to use it, or turn her away because the problem is essentially her fault? Give employees the ability to make decisions that build customer loyalty and satisfaction, and your clients will respond with repeat business.

HANDLING COMPLAINTS ABOUT STAFF

If you own a business or manage people, you're going to get occasional complaints from customers about someone on your staff. How you handle these situations sets important boundaries with your clients, while also opening up communication with your staff members.

It's important to take action on a customer's issue, but not by immediately terminating an employee. First, sit down with the staff member in question to find out his side of the situation. If there was a specific incident, get the breakdown of events and see where the interaction went wrong. It may be that a disciplinary action of some kind is warranted, but the issue may also be a simple misunderstanding, or an outburst triggered by the customer's behavior. If you have to make a change, do it with full knowledge of the circumstances—and with an understanding of the impact this will have on your relationship with your customer. No client should believe that you would leap to automatically fire someone on her orders.

IN THE END, YOU HAVE TO EAT

One of the toughest areas in which to set a limit is accounts receivable. Your business must collect money in exchange for its goods and services, or it won't be able to pay its employees or turn on the lights. Customers, however, have all kinds of issues with prompt payment: slow accounting departments, corporate policies that don't favor suppliers, bad cash flow, and unexpected expenses. When and how do you cut off their business until their bills are paid? The answer depends on the customer and his actual ability to pay. In large corporations, an invoice may have to work its way through a prehistoric system that processes them all in 60 to 75 days. In the case of small companies, however, you will want to set stricter limits to the time allowed for payment: A bill that is more than 30 days past due signals cash flow issues, and you're well within your rights to say, "I'm sorry, but I can't afford to continue to run up receivables with you. Once we receive payment for our invoices, we can resume business promptly."

"Let Me Speak to Your Supervisor"

FIRST, OFFER TO HELP

Some customers begin the conversation by demanding a supervisor, before you've had any opportunity to hear their issue. They may simply believe a supervisor will bring their issue to a faster resolution than a customer service rep, salesperson, or any other employee. You can certainly bring this person to your supervisor, but you may also be able to probe for more information first. A good response is, "I'd be happy to let Ms. Smith know you'd like to speak with her. But first, is there any way I can help? I may be able to save you some time." In some cases, the customer will be more than happy to tell you why she needs the supervisor, and you may be able to resolve the issue faster.

FOLLOW UP

Once the issue has been resolved to the customer's satisfaction, impress her further by following up by phone or e-mail to be certain that whatever promises your supervisor made have been fulfilled. If not, track down the bottleneck and make certain this customer receives what she expects. This re-establishes the credibility of your entire service operation, from the bottom up.

CLARIFY THE ISSUE

Why does the customer want to speak to someone with more authority? In some cases, this may be an intimidation tactic: He thinks that, if he threatens to go over your head, you'll believe he's going to complain about you to your boss, which could lead to you losing your job. This, he thinks, will make you capitulate and give him whatever he wants. You will have a greater impact if you respond with, "My supervisor is serving another customer right now. Perhaps I've misunderstood what you've said so far. What I've heard you say is . . ." You may reveal an actual misunderstanding, which can lead to resolution of the customer's issue.

DON'T TAKE THE BAIT

It's possible that the customer will not tell you why she wants a supervisor. She may even insult you: "No, I'm sick of dealing with stupid customer service people," or even, "I don't want to talk to someone who isn't from this country." You may feel the hairs rise on the back of your neck, but nothing will be accomplished by taking the bait. Smile and excuse yourself (or put the customer on hold) and find the supervisor. Later, you can congratulate yourself on your self-control.

BRIEF YOUR SUPERVISOR

You can help bring the situation to an expedient close if your supervisor already understands the problem before he picks up the phone or meets the customer. Let him know what the problem is in your own words, and he will then clarify things further with the client before moving toward a solution. Your customer will be relieved and, perhaps, even impressed that the supervisor knows what's going on before entering the discussion.

"THE DOCTOR ASKED ME TO CALL"

Few phrases are more powerful than this—the fact that the doctor feels something is important enough to bring to the patient's attention by phone. Even though the person calling is a nurse, a physician's assistant, or an office person, the doctor's gravitas is behind her words. Even if your business has nothing to do with medicine, you can use this same power to your advantage. Have a customer service rep make a call that begins with, "My manager (or supervisor, or the owner) has reviewed your issue and asked me to call you." This can bring a difficult matter to a swift resolution. The customer will know a higher-up is on top of his issue, which will make him think the proposed solution is the best he can get from your company.

Giving Away Extra

SURPRISES LEAD TO LOYALTY

On November 26, 2014, Verizon Wireless made an unprecedented gesture. Knowing that people would be shopping online in far greater numbers during the first week after Thanksgiving, the company dubbed the date "Connection Day" and gave customers of its More Everything data plan an additional gigabyte of data to use as they pleased—to stream audio and video, download audio books and movies, or do anything else they might want to do online. It also arranged special promotions with Amazon, Apple, Pandora, JetBlue, and others to make the extra data even more valuable. "As we approach the holidays, we wanted to give one of the first gifts of the season and show our customers how much we appreciate them," said Kristi Crum, president of the South Central Region of Verizon Wireless. Verizon's magnanimity may have cost it a day's revenue, but what it achieved in terms of customer loyalty most likely outweighed the outlay. (No doubt many customers of Sprint, T-Mobile, and AT&T raised their eyebrows that day, wondering why their service providers didn't do the same.)

HEAL A SLIGHT WITH A GIFT

One of the most practical tools in the customer service toolbox, a free service or gift provides an easy way to fix a problem when a customer calls with a complaint. Offering a free month of service, a gift card, or coupons for free products can make her feel like you've truly compensated her for her inconvenience. Create a list of items that customer service reps (and everyone else in your company) can use as an apologetic gesture to the customer. Their out-of-pocket cost can be quite low, especially when compared to the cost of finding new clients!

HOLIDAY GIFTS

Any company can give gifts to its customers for the December holidays. Small giveaways cement loyalty at a time of year in which consumer budgets are tight. Providing gift cards or free additional services or merchandise not only acknowledges your customers' patronage, but may also help them with their own gift giving. Ideally, they will feel that you've offered them something thoughtful and useful during what can be a stressful time of the year.

USE YOUR PARTNERSHIPS

If you have subsidiary companies or close associations with other brands, you have an opportunity to give them visibility through customer service giveaways. For example, Darden owns a number of restaurant chains, so it can offer gift cards and coupons for free menu items in several different chains—Olive Garden, Longhorn Steakhouse, Bahama Breeze, The Capital Grille, Seasons 52, and others.

WAIVE THE UPCHARGE

One thing that infuriates customers is a long list of tiny charges on their bill. While most customers understand that companies in some industries need to charge a variety of taxes on their goods and services, they can become irate when they see small fees for things like parts, ancillary equipment rental (like the wires required to run a carpet shampooing machine), or reports generated by the company's information systems. Consider offering one or more of these low-fee items for free, as a special perk of working with your company instead of a competitor.

USEFUL GIVEAWAYS ONLY

Customers appreciate the thought that goes into giveaways as much as they do the gift, item, or discount itself. With this in mind, be sure to offer them something they can actually use, or that reduces the cost of their purchase. "We're really sorry about your malfunctioning hard drive, but here's a T-shirt to make up for it," is hardly a ringing endorsement of your customer's importance to you. Make him feel valued by offering him something he will personally appreciate, and you will have taken a positive step toward retaining his patronage.

Providing Alternatives

MAKE OFFERS, BUT DON'T PUSH

"The most persuasive thing any [rep] can do is put the information out there," said Joe Crisara, CEO of ContractorSelling.com, in an interview for Field Service Digital. "The only influence you should have is by offering the solutions and maintaining your neutrality, so the customers don't feel like you're trying to push something. You lose credibility by recommending the top option; and if you recommend the bottom one, you insult people."

CHOICES SATISFY CUSTOMERS

When a customer contacts you with a problem, you may have more than one solution to offer. A variety of make-goods allows him to choose whichever one he values most. You could say something like, "While the company's policies don't provide for me to give you a full refund, I can offer you a credit for two months of service, or a $50 Visa gift card. Either of these would have similar value to a refund." The customer can then make a choice, and feel like he received both a good value and true acknowledgment of his issue.

FULFILL THE NEED

Whether you sell to customers or work with them to solve their complaints, you have the opportunity to fulfill their needs for certain products or services. Sometimes, this means you'll need to think quickly in order to offer them a substitute for the item they require. For example, say a customer comes into your store looking for a specific item at a specific price. You don't have that item, but you have one just like it from a different brand, for a slightly higher price. You have two options:

1. You can say, "I'm sorry, we don't carry that brand."
2. Or you can say, "We don't carry that particular brand, but we do have this one that has all the same features. It's a dollar higher in price, but it will certainly do the job."

The second answer offers the customer what she needs, with the benefit of immediate availability. She can continue to spend her time shopping, or she can leave with the item she requires right now.

OFFER PRICE ALTERNATIVES

Sometimes the service a customer requires costs money, because it involves repairing an item, purchasing an item to replace one that can't be repaired, or buying a one-time or ongoing service contract. In this case, the customer service representative must act as a salesperson as well. Have a series of alternatives to offer customers: contracts at different price points, replacement products with a range of features, or repairs that will work for the short or long term. Give clients options and allow them to choose, without attempting to push them in any particular direction.

PART

REAL-LIFE
SCENARIOS

How do you handle an irate customer at your counter or in your office? What do you say when she's just plain wrong? Equally important, how do you talk to her if she approaches you with a totally reasonable request you can't fulfill?

You will find answers to these and many other questions in what follows. We have gathered the advice of some of the most skilled customer relationship managers in the world, currently working for companies renowned for their service. The scenarios and solutions presented here are specific, but they apply to a wide variety of businesses. Whether you work for (or own) a micro-business, a midsize organization, or a corporation with call centers around the globe, you'll find this part of the book very helpful.

We give you the right words to use in many of the most common interactions with customers, as well as gestures of good faith, offers to soothe bristled feelings, and management advice on how to help employees understand their limits—and when to push them. Each suggestion has proved effective in the real world, which is ultimately where customer transactions will impact the state of your business.

HELP A CUSTOMER FIND INFORMATION

A customer calls a health insurance company to find out how to move his aging mother's insurance from a company in his current city to a different company in a new city. He needs to choose a new policy, but he does not have a clear understanding of Medicare and how it fits into the insurance picture.

WHAT TO DO: Say, "I will be happy to help you with that. It may take us 20 minutes or so to go through all the information. Do you have time now, or is there a better time for us to talk?" Find out what information the customer already has by asking simple questions. If he does not have all the information you need at that point, help him by suggesting where it may appear on forms available to him. Explain the various policies he can choose from, and how they are different. Help him make the right choice.

GIVE A LITTLE EXTRA

A customer comes into the restaurant where you work and orders a hamburger and a chocolate shake. She asks you for an extra pickle, and says, "I always ask for this, and the counter staff always give it to me."

WHAT TO DO: Give her the pickle, says Bob Farrell, customer service trainer in Seattle, Washington, who owned the restaurant in which this transaction took place. He came up with the Pickle Principle when a disappointed customer wrote to tell him that his counter staff had failed to give him his usual extra pickle. A pickle doesn't cost much, but it buys you a lot of customer satisfaction. "When something happens with a customer and you're not sure what to do, give 'em the pickle," he tells his clients. "Do what it takes to make things right."

LATE DELIVERY

When a package sent by FedEx from the East Coast to Minnesota arrives a full day later than "absolutely, positively overnight," the sender calls FedEx directly to complain. The service rep looks up the shipment and finds that the delay was caused by a mechanical error in an airplane, not by a weather system or other natural event. In other words, it was FedEx's fault.

WHAT TO DO: Apologize for the inconvenience and refund the customer's shipping costs in full. FedEx should stand behind its overnight guarantee, and a plane with engine trouble certainly counts as a circumstance for which the company is culpable. Take responsibility for your own mistakes.

AN IMPATIENT CUSTOMER

A customer comes into your restaurant at a particularly busy time of day. You take his name and the number of people in his party, and tell him it will be about 20 minutes until a table becomes available. Despite the obvious crowd of people waiting, the customer becomes more and more agitated, looking at his watch and returning to your station over and over to confirm his position on the waiting list. The second those 20 minutes expire, he comes over to your station and demands to know when you will seat him.

WHAT TO DO: First, set expectations accordingly. Keep an eye out for any problems in the dining room, so you can warn this obviously impatient customer if it looks like his wait will be longer than expected. Acknowledge his agitation and ask him if he only has a short time for his meal. Would he be willing to take a table that might involve a little crowding for his party? He may be willing to accept a little inconvenience to get in and out faster.

EXPLAINING COMPANY POLICY

A customer comes to your counter holding a plastic bag. Inside is a hairband made of tiny beads threaded on delicate strands of filament. You can see that at least two of the filaments are broken and the beads are loose in the bag. She tells you she knows it's her fault the filament broke, but she'd like a refund on the hairband. Your store's policy is no refunds on this particular style because the hairband is so delicate.

WHAT TO DO: Explain that while you can't offer her a refund, you can exchange this hairband for another one just like it. Show her a way to put on the hairband more gently. If she continues to push for a refund, offer her store credit for another item more to her liking.

KEEPING THE CUSTOMER WAITING WHILE YOU FIND AN ANSWER

You are in a live chat with a customer who is having a technical problem with her printer. The problem is not responding to the first or second solution you've offered, so you need to conduct further research on what other things to try. The customer needs to wait a few minutes while you do this.

WHAT TO DO: Set expectations by typing, "Let me see what additional steps we can take to help you. May I ask you to wait a few moments while I check my database?" If the customer responds that she doesn't want to wait, say, "I don't want to leave you without a solution. Is there a time later today when we can chat again?" If you can't arrange for her to contact you directly, be sure to save the entire content of the chat in the support center's system; that way, whoever takes over from you later will have the background knowledge to assist her more efficiently.

WHEN YOUR SUPERVISOR IS UNAVAILABLE

Your work in the call center at a satellite radio company, and a customer has called to convert his current service to his new car and radio. For no reason you can determine, the service will not port over in the usual way. The customer becomes angry and demands to speak with your supervisor. You ask him to wait while your supervisor is busy talking to another client. After 10 minutes, however, your supervisor still cannot extricate himself from that call.

WHAT TO DO: Say, "I know we haven't found a solution yet, but my supervisor is working with another customer and can't come to the phone. I want to make sure you get the help you need. What's the most convenient way to reach you? Once my supervisor is available, I'll make sure he calls you." Get the customer's phone number and available times to talk. As soon as your supervisor is available, provide him with all of the information about the call so far, and ask him to call the customer right away.

WHEN YOU DON'T KNOW THE ANSWER

You're working as a ticket clerk at a film festival. A patron approaches you with his 10-year-old daughter in tow and the festival program in his hand. He wants to know if the movie for which he is about to buy tickets contains profanity or nudity. You have not seen the movie and cannot judge if it's appropriate for children.

WHAT TO DO: Say, "I don't know, but I'll find out." Find a festival official and ask the question, then return as promptly as you can with an answer. If possible, stay with the patron and call the festival official on your cell phone.

WHEN VOLUME IS NO EXCUSE

You work for an executive recruitment company. When a job opportunity comes in, you place ads in a wide range of online sites and forums, and are flooded with applications. Your profession dictates a personal response to every candidate, but with five people on your staff and up to 500 applicants per position, you can't handle the volume. You send form letters to rejected applicants—but you're getting a lot of annoyed pushback from these candidates.

WHAT TO do: Instead of having to write hundreds of personal letters or e-mails, divide the candidates according to the reason you're rejecting them, and create a dozen or so different response letters. So, for example, if 40 applicants don't have the education level required by the client, send out a letter to them that specifically explains that they have been rejected for this reason. The candidates will know right away if they are included in the consideration set, and they will get individualized feedback about their candidacy. They will be more likely to submit their names again for another (more appropriate) position down the road.

AN UNAVAILABLE ITEM

You work in a jewelry store, and a customer contacts you with an interest in a specific style of Rolex watch. You'd love to make this lucrative sale, but the item won't be available for another month.

WHAT TO DO: Keep control of the sale by promising the customer that you will take the initiative. Tell her, "That product will be available on April 12. I can reserve one for you right now and give you a call as soon as it arrives."

A REQUEST TO BREAK THE RULES

You work in a resort hotel. A guest arrives with his entire family. He has a prepaid reservation, but he neglected to tell the hotel that he was bringing his dog with him. Your hotel has a strict "no pets" policy. He asks, "Can't you just let him stay here? He's really quiet and we'll keep him in the room and won't even let him bark."

WHAT TO DO: Your customer has put you in a difficult position, because he's already paid for his family's rooms. It will be up to you to make this work for him, and he knows it. Say, "Mr. Smith, I would love to help you, but we have this policy because pets always leave hair behind. We would have to steam-clean each room if a pet stayed in it—and that would result in very high additional fees for its owner. However, I know of several places right nearby where you can board your dog overnight and pick him up every day to take out on the beach with you. Let me make some calls to see which one has an opening."

YOUR COMPANY IS AT FAULT

A customer discovers an error in the software she bought from your company. She brings it to your attention, and you follow her steps on your computer and get the same result. The problem is clearly a bug.

WHAT TO DO: Thank the customer for finding this bug, and say, "I will get my technology people on this right away, so we can fix it and send out an update. On behalf of this company, I apologize for the inconvenience. I'm glad you decided to report it, so we can make it right."

A CUSTOMER RECEIVES A BROKEN PRODUCT

You're selling products through Amazon, which means all your sales are fulfilled by mail. You send a carefully packaged product to a customer, but when it arrives you get an angry message from her via Amazon's Seller Central messaging service, telling you the product arrived broken.

WHAT TO DO: You've sent dozens of items identical to this one, so you know the fault is not in the packaging or the product, but in something that happened after the item left your business. Blaming the U.S. Postal Service may be appropriate, but it doesn't help the customer. Instead, say, "I'm very sorry to hear this. It's so disappointing to receive a broken item. I will send you a new one today, along with postage-paid return packaging so you can send me the damaged item and I can research what went wrong." You're not pointing your finger at anyone, and you will receive proof of what happened in case you do want to pursue it with the post office.

THE SPREADING CUSTOMER

A customer brings her clothing selections to your counter for purchase. She confides to you under her breath that this is the first time she's had to buy plus-size clothing.

WHAT TO DO: Say, "If it looks great and you feel good wearing it, it makes no difference. No one else knows what size your clothes are. Wear it and know that you look beautiful."

THE STRANDED CUSTOMER

You are a Chicago customer service representative for an airline. It's a stormy day across the northern states, so flights are grounded and need to be rebooked. Customers line up at your counter; some of them are not going to make it out of O'Hare tonight. You don't have enough flights on your airline the next day to accommodate all of them.

WHAT TO DO: There are policies and procedures for this scenario, of course, but it's your attitude that will make the positive difference for these passengers. Say, "We are so sorry for this inconvenience, but we do need to make sure everyone is safe. We are looking at every alternative to accommodate you. We will work to get as many of you on alternate flights as we can. If we can't get you on a flight tomorrow, we will do our best to book you with another airline. Most importantly, we will keep you informed every step of the way, until you are headed to your destination."

WHEN THE CUSTOMER IS WRONG

You are the front desk person in the service department of a car dealership. An elderly customer comes in for a repair, and insists the problem with this car is the carburetor. The car is nearly new, however, and cars have not had carburetors since the twentieth century.

WHAT TO DO: Say, "Thank you for your suggestion. What you're describing can be caused by a number of different things, so I'll have our technicians check all of the systems. I will call you as soon as I know what the trouble is."

THE CUSTOMER WANTS TO TELL YOU HOW TO DO YOUR JOB

You work in a medical practice, and you are on the phone with a patient who is waiting for test results that may indicate a serious illness. His results have not arrived yet. He says, "Now you listen to me. Go tell the doctor that I want to know right now what the results are, and get her to call the lab and find out. Do it now!"

WHAT TO DO: Do your best not to get upset by the customer's tone. Smile—it will help you remain calm and sound friendly. Say, "Mr. Smith, I can only imagine how difficult this is for you. The fact is that this test requires a few days in laboratory conditions before the results are clear. I'm so sorry for the delay, but we should have the results by Friday. I will make absolutely sure the doctor calls you when they come in."

AN ANGRY CUSTOMER INSULTS YOU

A customer in your store is not satisfied with your response to her problem. She says, "You know what? You're an idiot. I don't know how you even got this job. Where's your manager? I want to talk to someone who's not mentally handicapped."

WHAT TO DO: Smile and say, "If you will wait here just a moment, I'll go and get my manager." Wait until you're out of visual and auditory range to have your very valid reaction to these insults. Take a moment to calm down, then go to your manager and provide the details of this interaction, including what the customer said to you. Return with the manager and stand by to fulfill whatever she and the customer agree should be done.

THE CUSTOMER WON'T LET
THE SUBJECT GO

A customer has e-mailed your business with a criticism of your website. You write back and thank her for the feedback, and explain where to find the information she needs. She writes to you again, and the new e-mail is a little angrier; she insists that the information should be on your site's landing page. You respond politely once more, thanking her for the suggestion. She writes a third time, and a fourth, and each e-mail is more angry and insulting than the one before it.

WHAT TO DO: Stop trying to explain. You are attempting to engage in conversation with someone who just wants angry confrontation, and is likely bringing in her rage over something else. Respond again with a brief, polite message; do not make further points that may prolong this argument. For example, you could say, "Thank you very much for your thoughts about this. I have forwarded your comments to our webmaster and our marketing staff. On behalf of our company, I wish you a pleasant day."

A CUSTOMER WISHES
SHE WERE THINNER

You work in a clothing store, and a customer insists on trying on clothes that are clearly two sizes too small. Nothing fits properly or looks good, but she can't seem to see what the problem is.

WHAT TO DO: Say, "You know, that looks uncomfortable, and that style runs really small. You might find the next size up to be much more flattering, and you will have a little more breathing room. Would you like me to get that for you?"

THE CUSTOMER IS PANICKED

You work in a call center, and a customer who uses your software products calls in a panic: He accidentally clicked on "Clear All" in his mail program, and lost his entire contact list—which he says contained some 2,000 contacts. He is desperate to find out if they can be retrieved.

WHAT TO DO: First, empathize. Say, "Wow, you must have been really upset when you saw that happen!" Then begin to find a solution: "Yes, we can get the list back. It's actually still on your hard drive." At this early point in the call, while the customer is on the verge of hyperventilating, do not suggest that he should be backing up his data to an external drive or the cloud. Do this at the very end, once his contact list has been restored.

THE CUSTOMER HAS TAKEN THE WRONG STEPS

You work for an insurance company, and a customer calls for assistance with a claim. When you look up his policy, you see that there are gaps in the necessary information. It appears that he has not filled out the right forms, and that his coverage may be in jeopardy because of it.

WHAT TO DO: Empathize, then guide the customer through your company's process. Say, "Mr. Smith, I'm sorry about this, as I know you're calling at a difficult time. It looks like there is some information missing on your policy. We'll need to complete that information before we file your claim. We can do this together by phone, or I can tell you where to find the forms online. I want to be sure all of this is complete so there will be no problem with your claim. Do you have a few minutes now to go through this?"

AN ESTATE EXECUTOR CALLS

You work for a wireless services company, and a man calls to turn off his mother's service. He tells you he is the executor of her will, and that she recently died. You know you will need a copy of her death certificate to turn off her service.

WHAT TO DO: First, acknowledge the death: "I am very sorry for your loss, Mr. Smith." Then be ready with the information he needs to expedite this cancellation. "I can tell you exactly what you need to do. I'll give you our fax number, and you'll need to fax us the death certificate, the page of the will indicating that you are the executor, and your mother's most recent invoice. Then we can get this service turned off promptly." This is not the time to attempt to sell him anything; treat the family of the deceased with respect and kindness.

A CUSTOMER BRINGS A NEW PROBLEM TO YOUR ATTENTION

A customer comes into your store with five laptops he bought several weeks before. The laptops have been in use in his office, but now he can't get any of them to power up. The laptops were expensive, and he is angry about having to deal with this.

WHAT TO DO: Apologize, and make it clear that you will help. "I am so sorry about this. I apologize for the inconvenience, and I want you to know that it's just as important to me to identify the problem as it is to you. Let's get these laptops to our technology experts and see what may be going on there. In the meantime, I'd like to minimize the inconvenience for you. What can we do to help you out over the next few days?"

SERVICE IS TAKING A LONG TIME, AND THE CUSTOMER IS ANGRY

You're on the phone with a customer who has a complicated technical problem. The phone call is taking a long time, because there are many steps to the solution. The customer finally gets frustrated and says, "You couldn't care less about me and my problem. I'm paying for this service contract—why can't you help me?"

WHAT TO DO: Don't escalate the sudden conflict. Say, "I know it's frustrating when you don't get the help you need right away. I'm sorry it's taking so long, but this particular issue is complex, so it's going to take a little while to fix. Please stick with me, and we will get this right."

THE HURRIED CUSTOMER

A customer enters your restaurant and tells you he and his family have theater tickets for this evening. They have limited time to have dinner before the event.

WHAT TO DO: Know which items on the menu can be served quickly. For example, the server could suggest the prime rib, or a baked potato and vegetables—items that are ready to go in most restaurants. The customer will appreciate the opportunity to have a good meal and still get out on time.

THE CUSTOMER IS SICK OF BEING PASSED AROUND

You work for a large bureaucracy. A customer reaches you after talking to six other people in your organization who could not help her. Now she's angry, and her first words to you are, "Okay, you are the seventh person I've talked to today. If you can't help me, I'm going to cancel my contract with you." You have no notes about her issue, so she has to repeat her whole story again.

WHAT TO DO: Start by acknowledging her frustration. "It's so distressing to get passed from one person to another. I do hope that I can be the last one! Tell me about your situation, and I will do my best to resolve it for you." If it turns out that you need to pass her to another office, make sure to also pass her information along so she does not have to repeat it all one more time.

THE CUSTOMER WANTS AN ARGUMENT

You connect with a caller who is already angry before your conversation begins. He begins by lecturing you about his problems with your company's products, and accusing the company of scams and conspiracies. Before you've had the opportunity to say much beyond "Good morning," he begins attacking you because you speak with an accent different from his.

WHAT TO DO: Make your own voice sound as neutral as possible. This caller wants you to get upset so he has more justification for his anger. Listen passively, and make empathetic sounds: "Mmm. I see. Yes, that's upsetting." If you take all the emotion out of your voice and respond calmly, he will eventually calm down, and you may have the opportunity to actually help him.

MEETING ANGER WITH KINDNESS

You work for a car insurance company, and a customer has been in a fender bender. He expected a claims adjuster to come to his home to look at the car and provide an estimate, but the adjuster hasn't called to make an appointment yet. The damage is just about enough to make the car look terrible, and driving it uncomfortable. The customer is frustrated, so now he wants to tell you everything that's wrong with your organization.

WHAT TO DO: Take the feedback and thank him for it. "I appreciate you sharing all of this with me. We need our customers to tell us when something isn't right, so we can take the necessary steps to fix it. Let me find out what the problem is with our representative, and I'll get him to call you as soon as possible." The customer does not expect you to be kind, so your calm, helpful tone will help defuse his anger.

THE MYSTERY PROBLEM

You are the service manager for a car dealership. A customer comes in with the car she bought last month. She says she hears a noise when she steps on the brakes, and wants it fixed. She describes the noise to you, but you can't think what might be causing it.

WHAT TO DO: Take a test drive with the customer before attempting repairs. Listen out for what she hears so you can determine what might be wrong on the first try. If the customer has never driven this model before, she may be hearing a normal function that she interprets as "something wrong." In this scenario, she very well may hear the anti-lock brakes working when she steps on the pedal—an unfamiliar but perfectly normal sound.

THE DISCOUNTED SERVICE

A customer buys a Groupon for carpet cleaning. He makes the appointment, the crew comes, and he leaves the house while they do the job. When he returns, he finds a large spot on one carpet, a stain he expected the company to remove. He calls to complain.

WHAT TO DO: Every person who buys a Groupon and uses your service for the first time has the potential to become a regular customer. Equally important, no customer should feel as if they are receiving half-price service because they didn't pay your full rate. In this case, send a manager to the home to look at the stain and determine what can be done to remove it. You may need to swallow the cost of a second service in order to ensure this customer is completely satisfied and tells his friends what a great job your company did for him.

AN INCORRECT INVOICE

A customer in your restaurant receives the check at the end of her meal. There's a charge on it she wasn't expecting, because the server did not tell her that her choice of side dish required an upcharge.

WHAT TO DO: Thank her for bringing the issue to your attention. Calmly explain to her that there is an additional charge for the item. If she balks at this, you can make the generous decision to take the charge off her bill because she was not informed of it. Tell her that you will also talk to the server about the issue so it doesn't happen again.

SLOW SERVICE

A customer and his friends are seated at a table in your restaurant. After 10 minutes, no one has approached them to offer them a beverage or take their order. The customer waves you over and tells you this.

WHAT TO DO: Apologize for the wait and take their beverage order. It's up to you whether you wish to pass that order on to the server or bring it yourself, but make sure this table gets their beverages and that service is prompt from this point forward. If there is a larger issue—for example, if the server has become ill or had an injury—explain this to the customers so they understand that this is an unusual situation, and that your restaurant always works hard to provide excellent service.

ERRORS IN THE ORDER

Customers at a table in your restaurant receive their respective orders, but there's an issue with one of them. Perhaps the steak is overdone, or it has been paired with the wrong side dish. When the server comes around to ask how everything is, the affected customer explains.

WHAT TO DO: Apologize and offer to take her plate back to the kitchen to correct the order. If she does not want to wait for a new plate while the rest of her party are eating, offer to bring her something in the interim that can be served right away (a cup of soup or a salad, for example). Make sure she's not charged for this extra item.

THE ORDER DOESN'T COME

On a busy day in your restaurant, you spot a table of customers who have not received their order in a timely manner.

WHAT TO DO: Check with the customers to see how long they have been waiting. Tell them you will follow up with their server to see what's going on. Do what you said you would do: Check with the server and the kitchen, and determine what the problem is. If it turns out the wait will be longer still (say, if the server did not enter the order correctly in the system), go back to the table, apologize for the wait, and offer everyone a complimentary item for their trouble: a glass of wine, perhaps, or an appetizer that can be served right away. Keep this table on your radar, and check in with the kitchen to be sure their order is in progress.

SETTING EXPECTATIONS

You sell cars at a dealership. You've closed a deal with a customer at the beginning of a new model year, so the car he purchased must be ordered for him. You tell him it will arrive in 10 days, but nine days later, there's no information on its status. The customer is expecting to stop by the next morning and take it home.

WHAT TO DO: Find out why the car has not arrived. Call the customer and tell him that you're keeping track of his order; fill him in on exactly where the car is and when it will be delivered. Even though it's not your fault, apologize on behalf of your company and the manufacturer. Say, "We never want to disappoint a customer, so I will keep track of this order and keep you informed of the expected delivery date." Then, do what you said: Check the delivery information regularly, and let the customer know where the car is as you find out more.

YOU NO LONGER CARRY A CUSTOMER'S FAVORITE ITEM

A customer who frequents your store comes in for her accustomed pack of cigarettes. Your store's management, however, has decided that selling cigarettes is counter to the store's stated mission of good health for all, so you no longer carry them. The customer becomes testy about this.

WHAT TO DO: Apologize, and direct her to a store at which she can purchase the item. Don't lecture her on the detrimental effects of smoking. Say, "I'm sorry to disappoint you, but we just don't sell cigarettes anymore. It's a new company policy. I hate to send you to another store, but I know that XYZ Pharmacy across the street still sells them. I hope we will continue to see you here for all of your other shopping."

AN ANGRY CUSTOMER CALLS

You receive a call from a customer who is already angry when you click in. He doesn't want to give you all the usual information— name, address, e-mail address, phone number—and just keeps shouting out his problem at you.

WHAT TO DO: Listen to the problem, and say, "Yes, sir, I can definitely help you with that. You will get the answer you need on this call. But first, please give me your phone number so I can call you back if we get disconnected." Once you've solved the problem, the customer will be much more willing to provide the rest of the information you need. If he hangs up, you have the option of calling him back, or checking the number in your database to see if the rest of his information is there.

YOUR PREVIOUS CUSTOMER UPSET YOU

You've just gotten off a call with an irate customer, and you need to take the next call right away. The last caller verbally assaulted your character and your competency. The next caller speaks calmly and has a simpler problem.

WHAT TO DO: Pause, take a deep breath, and smile—putting a smile on your face will help you and your voice relax. Remember that this next call has nothing whatsoever to do with the last one. Treat this new caller with the respect due to her. (See Part Five for more on this.)

THE CALL THAT WON'T END

You work in a department that offers technical service, and the call you've been on with a customer seems to be taking forever. The caller does not understand the technology—in fact, it sounds like this is his first computer—so you're walking him through the process step by step.

WHAT TO DO: There's a reason patience is a virtue. It's also a skill, and your calm, methodical approach will help you solve the issue to everyone's satisfaction. Listen carefully to what the customer is telling you, and see if you can find the roadblock between his understanding of the device and the proper way to use it. It may be that he does not understand the vocabulary you are using, or that he is calling a part of the product by the wrong name. Detecting issues like these can turn a prolonged call into a fairly simple problem.

IT'S NOT IN STOCK

A customer comes into your store looking for a specific item. Normally you stock this item, but today it's out of stock and it will be days before the next shipment arrives. The customer needs it today for a child's birthday party.

WHAT TO DO: If your store is part of a chain, call other stores in your network to see if they have the item in stock. If they do not, call the competition and see if they've got it. Have one put aside for the customer, and send her to the store that has the item. You may lose this one sale, but you will gain the respect and gratitude of this customer, and you can be sure she will come to your store again.

THE ITEM IS BURIED IN THE STOCK ROOM

A customer comes to your store looking for a specific item he has seen there before. The item is not on the sales floor, but your system says a shipment has arrived in the last day. It's going to take a while to find it.

WHAT TO DO: Ask for the customer's mobile phone number. Tell him you will check for the item in the new shipment and you will call him as soon as you find it. This allows him to continue shopping or running other errands while you search, or while your stock workers unpack the shipment. As soon as you have the item in hand, call the client to come back for it, and leave it at your customer service desk in his name.

SELLING THE BEST ITEM FOR THE CUSTOMER

A customer comes into your hardware store looking for new compact fluorescent (CFL) light bulbs to replace her old-fashioned incandescent light bulbs. She does not know much about CFL bulbs, and immediately reaches for the most expensive one.

WHAT TO DO: You have knowledge that the customer does not, so apply it to this situation. Ask her what fixtures the bulbs will be used in, and make recommendations based on her answers. When the most expensive bulb is not the best choice, let her know and recommend a cheaper one. This response is a win for everyone: You demonstrate your expertise, the customer buys a range of bulbs for different lights, and you build trust because you did not steer her toward the more expensive choice.

THE OUTDATED WARRANTY

A customer comes into your store with an item he purchased a little over six months earlier. The item no longer works, apparently through no fault of his own, but its warranty has expired.

WHAT TO DO: First, apologize to the customer for the inconvenience. Take the item back, and offer him store credit. Take up the issue with the manufacturer, not with the customer. The manufacturer will want to know that its product has failed just six months after purchase, as this may signal a larger problem in the manufacturing process.

LOCATING A LOST ITEM

A customer leaves her wallet in your store. The store policy is to leave the wallet in the lost-and-found box at the store and wait for her to call for it.

WHAT TO DO: If there is identification in the wallet, call the owner and let her know you have it. Attach a note that lets the rest of the staff know the customer has been contacted and will come by to pick it up. Place the item in a secure location and let the manager know where it is, so she can retrieve it promptly with its contents intact. You have alleviated a lot of anxiety for the customer, who will remember your kindness and tell her friends about how nicely you handled the situation.

THE CUSTOMER NEEDS IT NOW

A customer comes into your store looking for an item you do not have in stock. You offer to order it, but he explains that he's leaving for South America at the end of the week and needs it today.

WHAT TO DO: Call other stores in your network to see if they have the item. If they do not, call the manufacturer and see about getting one sent out that day for overnight or two-day delivery. Keep an eye on this order online, to be sure it ships in the time frame you promised the customer. If anything seems to be delayed, inform him right away.

THE WRONG PRICE

A customer brings an item to your register, and when it rings up, she says, "No, that's not what the pricing said on the shelf [or on the tag]."

WHAT TO DO: Check the pricing on the shelf or tag, and if the price is lower than the register's price, give the customer the lower price. The store made the error, so she should receive the price she expected. In many states, you are obliged by law to charge the price on the shelf label or price tag, and consumers know this. (Be sure to correct the error as soon as she leaves the store.)

A DISAPPEARING PACKAGE

A customer alerts you through your website that he got a message from you saying his package had been delivered, but that he doesn't have it. It may have been stolen from his porch.

WHAT TO DO: Send the customer a new package at no additional charge—not even for the shipping. If no one saw it being boosted from his home, there will never be a way to know what happened to it. Lack of delivery is not the customer's fault. It's not your fault either, but you can take that up with the shipping company, especially if the shipment was insured. Keeping the customer is worth the cost of a new item.

THE TWEET

A customer tweets that she misses a product your stores used to carry. She does you the courtesy of tweeting this to your Twitter handle, so you can spot it quickly.

WHAT TO DO: First, let the customer know you saw the tweet by responding to it with a question: "@SunshineJane, was it the Black and Decker 4705 weed trimmer?" Then check into the reason the product was discontinued, and let her know: "@SunshineJane, B&D stopped making that one, but we still have the line refills in stock. Come on in!" The fast, personal response will impress her, and—most importantly—she will get what she needs.

PHONE VERSUS PERSON

Your business telephone rings just as a customer walks up to your counter.

WHAT TO DO: The customer standing in front of you always outranks the person on the other end of the phone. If there is no one else to answer, pick up the call and ask the caller to hold while you finish your business. It's good to have a phone that notes the numbers of the calls you've received, so you can return them promptly even if the person on the other end does not choose to hold. Call him back as soon as you can. Your quick callback will impress him, especially if you begin with, "I'm sorry I missed your call. I was with another customer when the phone rang."

THE CUSTOMER DISLIKED
BEING ON HOLD

*A customer calls your store, and you ask her if you can put her
on hold while you deal with a customer who is there in person.
When you pick up the line several minutes later, she is angry
about having been on hold for so long.*

WHAT TO DO: Apologize for the delay. Say, "I'm sorry you
had to wait. I had a customer here at the register, and it took
a few minutes to take care of him. How can I help you?" The
customer may still be testy, but your apology and quick service
will help improve her mood.

THE CUSTOMER DIDN'T GIVE YOU
ALL THE INFORMATION

*A customer orders a meal in your restaurant. When the meal
comes, he looks at the sauce on the plate and asks, "Does this
have chicken broth in it? I'm a vegetarian."*

WHAT TO DO: If the dish does indeed have a meat broth,
take the plate away and apologize to the customer, even though
this is not your restaurant's fault. Offer to bring something that
can be served right away—a salad or appetizer, perhaps—so he's
not sitting with an empty place setting while others in his group
are eating. Bring him a menu so he can choose another dish.
If your menu does not indicate which meals are vegetarian, it's
a good idea to change that in order to avoid this kind of issue in
the future.

THE CUSTOMER DOESN'T HAVE TIME TO WAIT FOR HIS MEAL

A customer orders a meal in your restaurant, but because of the high volume of patrons at this particular hour, her meal is delayed and she can no longer wait for it.

WHAT TO DO: Apologize to the customer for the wait. Offer to package the meal to go. If the meal is not ready, offer an alternative: one or more items that can be served immediately. Don't let her leave hungry, as she will always and forever associate this feeling with your establishment. If she is angry, offer her a discount on whatever meal she takes with her—and if she must leave empty-handed, don't try to charge her for the meal.

THE FAMILY OF THE PATIENT

You are a healthcare worker in a rehabilitation center. A patient's adult daughter comes to the nurses' station. You haven't seen her before, so you don't know which patient is her mother. She tells you she has just flown in from another state and has been calling the doctor and the nurses' station for days, but no one has returned her calls. She doesn't know a single thing about her mother's condition and is frantic with worry.

WHAT TO DO: It doesn't matter if you're not that patient's nurse; the organization has truly dropped the ball for this family. There's no point in getting defensive—the daughter will perceive it as yet another obstacle to her search for information. First, empathize and apologize on behalf of the entire facility. "Oh, my! I am so sorry no one has been in contact with you. You must be worried sick about your mother. Please tell me her name, and let's see what I can tell you about her condition. I'll also page the doctor for you, so you can get the whole picture."

THE BOTCHED DELIVERY

You work for a delivery company, and a shipping customer calls. Her product is glass bells, and she ships dozens of these every day. One of her clients has called to tell her that a product arrived in a damaged state. She's never had breakage before, so she wants to know what went wrong and how she can get the shipping cost refunded.

WHAT TO DO: Apologize to the customer for the inconvenience, and explain that you will need to research the issue in order to determine exactly what went wrong. Take her through the process of filing a claim. Set reasonable expectations about what will happen next. Be clear on the amount of research and processing time that will elapse before she receives a response about her claim, and tell her how she will receive this response. This is not the time to suggest to her that her packaging may have been faulty; you don't yet know anything more than she does about what may have happened to her package.

THE SPECIAL GIFT

You ship an item to a customer—a discontinued collectible he planned to give to his mother for her birthday. It was the last in your inventory, and it arrived damaged. He calls in a panic.

WHAT TO DO: Chances are you know which wholesale clients might have this item in their stock. Apologize to the customer and tell him you will make some calls to locate another item, and that you will keep in touch to let him know of your progress. Get the item shipped to him overnight at your expense. If the item truly can't be found, offer him another item at no charge, as your gift to him.

THE COMPLICATED REPAIR

A customer comes into your car repair shop with a problem that sounds to you and your technicians like it's the camshaft. You replace the camshaft, and the problem seems to go away. A week later, the customer is back to report that it has actually gotten worse. You discover that your technicians installed the camshaft incorrectly, so you replace it again. Still, the problem persists, and the customer returns for a third time.

WHAT TO DO: Tell him that you will take a harder look at this problem, and you will get to the bottom of it. Do your best to determine what's really gone wrong. When you find the actual problem, charge the customer for the corresponding parts, but not for the labor. Be sure to apologize for the inconvenience, and for your own mistakes throughout the process.

THE RENTAL RESERVATION

You work at a car rental company in an airport. A customer comes to the counter much later than expected. Her flight was late, and, in the interim, the model and size of car she reserved has been rented to other customers. You no longer have the size she would like.

WHAT TO DO: You risk starring in a scene out of a *Seinfeld* episode here, so be sure to satisfy your customer. Apologize for the omission, and refrain from suggesting that the real problem is that she's late—she is already annoyed enough about this, and the situation was out of her control. Offer an upgrade: a vehicle the next size up at no extra charge. Chances are she will take it and actually see it as an advantage.

THE DIRTY ROOM

You work at the registration desk in a budget hotel. A customer checks in after 6 p.m., but when he goes to his room, it looks to him as if it has not been cleaned properly.

WHAT TO DO: It does not matter if the room has indeed been cleaned—if your housekeeping staff did a substandard job, you may have an issue to solve later. If you have another room, offer it immediately, and also offer to help the customer move his luggage so he can be comfortable in a clean room as quickly as possible.

THE UNSERVICED ROOM

A guest at your hotel returns to her room late in the evening after a long work day. As soon as she enters her room, she calls the front desk to report that it has not been serviced. The bed isn't made, her towels are in a heap on the floor, and there's dirt on the carpet.

WHAT TO DO: If there is no other staff member on duty who can clean the room, there's no way around it—it's up to you. Grab towels, sheets, and a cart and go clean up. If this is simply not feasible because you need to stay at the front desk, offer the guest a different room that you know to be clean, and help her move her luggage so she can make an easy transition. Don't discuss your internal problems with the guest; just tell her that you will look into the situation and you're very sorry that she had to come back to a dirty room.

THE LATE CHECK-IN

A guest arrives at your hotel much later than planned, and you no longer have a room of the size he requested, with the amenities he expected. It's your company's policy that you do not guarantee special requests. The guest tells you he's terribly disappointed and that he does not know if he still wants to stay here, although it's much too late for him to cancel his reservation.

WHAT TO DO: First, apologize for the lack of availability, and ask questions about the guest's needs. For example, perhaps he wanted a ground floor room because it would make it easier for him to bring in his luggage, or needed a large desk because he has a presentation to prepare for the next day. Offer several other options that may meet his needs. Maybe you can offer him a workspace somewhere else in the hotel, or a suite with a table he can use. You can compensate him with complimentary meals in your hotel restaurant, or a room with different amenities (like a Jacuzzi suite) at no extra charge. Give him choices, so he can select whatever suits him best.

NOT YOUR JOB

You are a stock person in a department store. A customer approaches you and asks if you would ring up her purchases.

WHAT TO DO: Say, "Let me find someone for you who can do that. I wish I could, but I'm not trained for that. Would you follow me?" Take the customer to a salesperson who can complete the transaction for her.

NOT YOUR EXPERTISE

You are an advertising agency account executive. You're in a meeting with a client, and he begins asking you questions about creative and production processes that are outside of your expertise.

WHAT TO DO: It may be your instinct to try to answer these questions on the spot, but you will probably lack the correct information. Say, "Do you mind if I take notes? Let me get all of your questions about that, and I'll take them back to the experts on our staff. I can get you the answers later today."

THE CUSTOMER HAD AN ACCIDENT

You are an optometrist with your own eyewear business. A customer comes in with a pair of glasses she wore while working in a machine shop. The glasses got sprayed with a solvent that ruined the lenses. She needs a new pair, but these are outside of the manufacturer's warranty.

WHAT TO DO: The issue is in no way your fault, but the customer had an accident and needs your help. First, show concern by asking if her eyes and face were injured, and if she needs or needed medical care. Deal with the glasses by coming up with the best discount you can for replacement lenses, keeping the same frames. Research this with the manufacturer to see if the company is willing to work with you on a special-case deal, or even if they would replace the lenses for free. You may be pleasantly surprised by the manufacturer's willingness to help you make this situation better.

THE JOSTLED BAGGAGE

You manage a hotel, and you call a bellman to take a guest's luggage to his room. Before his bags even leave the lobby, the bellman has a mishap and drops them off the cart. The guest becomes frantic with worry that something may be broken.

WHAT TO DO: First, show concern for the guest's property. Go over yourself to help the bellman get the bags back on the cart, and assure the guest that you will cover the cost if anything inside is damaged. Say, "Let's get the bags up to your room, where you can check to see if everything's all right. If not, call down to me right away, and we'll take care of it." You probably have a process for handling guests' damage claims, so be prepared to handle this quickly if something was indeed broken.

A GUEST HAS AN EMERGENCY CHECKOUT

You are a manager at a hotel in a resort area. It's your busiest week of the year, so prices are high and your hotel is packed. On the morning after a big event, a guest comes to the desk with red eyes, and tells you that she's just had word that her father has died. She has to check out right away.

WHAT TO DO: First, say, "I am so sorry for your loss." Handle the checkout smoothly, and don't charge her for the remaining days on her reservation. Even if you suspect she's trying to get out of a longer stay, take her word for it that she has had a death in the family. If she hasn't, you've lost a few days of a booking—but if she has, you've gained a fan for life who will tell the story to her friends and family, and speak highly of your hotel for years to come.

THE TERRIBLE, AWFUL DAY

You work evenings at a store, and you've already had a day that will go down in history as a new record as far as miserable days go. You arrive at your evening job feeling angry and resentful that you have to work tonight of all nights.

WHAT TO DO: No one you will meet this evening has anything to do with your bad day, so don't punish them for your experience. Take a deep breath, put a smile on your face, and treat customers the way they deserve to be treated. You may find that your mood lifts as your evening progresses—and at the very least, you won't feel any worse than you did when you came in.

COMMUNICATING WITH THE HARD OF HEARING

A person comes into your store wearing a hearing aid. He speaks to you, but you have trouble understanding his words. He also uses sign language, but you don't have that skill.

WHAT TO DO: Get out a pad and a pen and hand them to him, so he can write what he needs. Alternately, have him type it out on his smartphone (or yours, if he doesn't have one) and show it to you. It's fine to write down or text your response as well. If he's looking for something specific, take him to the corresponding shelf, pick up the item, and look at him to see if that's what he wanted.

Above all else, don't shout at him or get annoyed with him because he can't communicate the way you normally would. He wants to communicate just as much as anyone else, and will thank you for your patience and your courtesy.

THE FAILED CAKE

You own a bakery, and a customer orders a cake with an icing message on top. You write down the order: "Best Wishes Francis, and underneath that, Good Luck in Your New Job." When the customer comes in to pick up the cake, you pull it out of the cooler and discover that your new pastry assistant has written:

Best Wishes Francis
And Underneath That
Good Luck in Your New Job

WHAT TO DO: Apologize and hope your customer has a sense of humor (and know that if he has a smartphone, he will take a picture, post it online and tell his friends). There's nothing to do but remove the writing and re-frost the cake with the correct inscription. Wait until the customer leaves to take this up with the staff member responsible for transcribing your instructions—and take a look at your internal process to prevent this from happening again.

THE UNEXPECTED GUEST

You are a server in a restaurant, and you bring two customers their salads. Before you've taken more than a few steps away from the table, one of the customers screams. A spider has just crawled out from under the lettuce leaves.

WHAT TO DO: Whisk away the salads immediately. Apologize, and don't try to make excuses (nothing sounds lamer than, "Well, you know, where there's food, there are bugs"). Offer the customer anything else she would like from the menu with the compliments of the management. If she does not throw down her napkin and run from the restaurant, have the manager come over and apologize as well.

THE OVERBEARING PARENT

You are a portrait photographer, and you're taking senior pictures for a young woman about to graduate from high school. The customer and her mother can see the portraits on your computer screen before you do any Photoshop work on them or make prints, so they can make sure they like their selection. No matter what poses your customer strikes or how many shots you take, however, her mother isn't happy.

WHAT TO DO: Be clear upfront about how many poses and frames you will shoot for a certain price, to give yourself the option of cutting off the session. Before you resort to this, however, suggest to the mother that her daughter should choose the photo she wants. If all else fails, tell the mother that you will be happy to shoot as many different poses or outfits as she'd like, but that there will be an additional charge after a certain number. This may bring the matter to a quick close.

THE UNATTENDED CHILD

You are a flight attendant on a major airline. A passenger approaches you to tell you that a 10-year-old flying alone is seated next to her, and he will not stop bouncing in his seat and yelling.

WHAT TO DO: The parents have made the airline responsible for the child's behavior. Take a few minutes to engage him in conversation, and see if you can find a way to distract him with an interesting pastime or task. Find out if he's carrying a book, crayons, or even a video game that he can play instead of bothering the adults on either side of him. At the very least, he will feel important because you gave him some attention; at best, you may be able to calm him down and alleviate the boredom that may be causing his behavior. If all else fails, switch him to the aisle seat so he can see you keeping an eye on him.

A SAFETY QUESTION

You are a flight attendant, and there's an unusual issue with condensation leaking from some vents on your flight. It's dripping on the passengers in that part of the plane. One of these passengers approaches you with concerns that something is wrong with the plane.

WHAT TO DO: Calm the passenger by explaining that the airline's management knows about the condensation problem, and that they would never allow the plane to leave the ground if they believed it was in any way dangerous. Say that you will report the issue, however, as it is interfering with the quality of the flight for this passenger and others. Check the area to see if there is a way to keep water from dripping on them, and move them out of those seats, if possible.

"A PIECE OF CRAP"

You work for a cellular phone provider. A customer comes into the store with a nearly new phone that has stopped working for no apparent reason. She is annoyed and frustrated to have her expensive phone malfunction so quickly, and when she approaches you, she waves it in your face and tells you it's "a piece of crap."

WHAT TO DO: Start with an apology. Say, "Oh, I'm so sorry about that. Let's find out if we can take care of the problem right away, and if not, we'll get you a new one." Let her tell you the entire sad story of the phone's failure, and take careful notes. Because the phone is under warranty, you can replace it right away if your examination doesn't result in an easy fix. Make sure the customer gets her cellular service up and running on the new phone before she leaves the store.

YOUR RUDE EMPLOYEE

You run a neighborhood hardware store. A customer approaches you and asks if you are the manager or owner. When you say that you are, he gives you an earful about an employee who has been rude to him.

WHAT TO DO: Take the customer's account of the situation seriously, and listen to all of it. Keep in mind that his description of what happened may be absolutely accurate, or it may be tempered by his perception of the event. Apologize for his bad experience, and offer to help him personally with whatever he needs from the store. After you have helped him, take the employee aside—out of earshot of your other customers—and hear her side of the story before you determine whether you need to take disciplinary action.

PART

CRISIS
MANAGEMENT

You've seen countless examples of customer service people in crisis on Facebook, Twitter, YouTube, and other social networking sites: the angry customer screaming at a salesperson, the nearly apoplectic cable television user shouting down a call center employee, the clearly delusional fast food customer hurling racial epithets at the counter help. These are the worst situations for people who serve customers, and they can be miserably difficult to defuse.

In this part of the book, we'll look at ways to handle moments like these. When you know how to deal with the worst that customers can dish out, you will be able to deflect hurtful criticism and graciously accept anger that may be aimed in your direction but is meant for someone else—probably someone well above your pay grade. You will also understand how to accept responsibility for an honest mistake and make the situation right for your customer.

Perhaps toughest of all are the times when employees must face angry customers after the company's top management has made a controversial statement or implemented an unwelcome policy. Higher-ups' unpopular decisions and mistakes tend to affect those on their payroll a lot more than they affect them.

Most of the scenarios described in this part involve isolated, short-term issues faced by individual customer service representatives, or by small business owners dealing with a single crisis. But customer service people also work on the front lines of crises that affect thousands or even millions of people: examples include the workers for charities who bring assistance to people in storm-ravaged areas; the reps taking calls from frantic consumers who just found out their spinach may contain dangerous bacteria; or the ones who must explain to callers that their credit card information may have been stolen.

What happens when real disaster strikes a large company? At the end of this part are stories from some of the most talked-about and long-term customer service crises in recent history. Some of these could not have been foreseen, while others were brought about by the companies themselves, through their failure to respond appropriately to individual customers.

No matter the size of your own business or your position within the company, you can learn from what the big companies did—or didn't do—when the going got tough.

All of these difficult circumstances require consummate skill in handling members of the general public. At the end of this part, we'll explore some of the most unusual and volatile cases. It's likely you will recognize some of the more famous public relations crises that became (or could have become) customer service nightmares. Whether you own your own company or you work in a call center for a major conglomerate, you can learn some important customer service skills from these case studies.

Extreme Anger

OUT-OF-CONTROL ANGER

When a customer approaches you with boiling rage, your best course of action is to become as calm and impassive as you can. Hold your own emotions in check, and turn a sympathetic ear to her as she raises her voice. In most cases, her anger will play itself out in a few minutes, but she won't be able to hear any response you make until it has peaked and starts to run down. Show concern, make eye contact if you can (many angry people pace or wave their arms, making eye contact difficult), and show that you are listening by responding with neutral sounds ("Mmmm, I see"). Once the customer has the worst of her anger behind her, you can move on to problem solving.

ANGER IN THE SHOWROOM

If an angry customer approaches you in the middle of your busy store, do your best to move him out of this environment as quickly as you can. Drawing a crowd will only fuel his anger, and it certainly won't help your business to have onlookers there while you try to calm him down. Say quietly, "I will be happy to listen to you, but we need to move over here," and maneuver him into an office, dressing room, or some other less exposed area. If he truly won't budge, he's looking to make a scene—which is another kind of crisis.

A CUSTOMER MAKING A SCENE

If a customer steps into the middle of your store and starts yelling at the top of her lungs, you have a different kind of situation on your hands. A person with the authority to act needs to approach this customer to determine what she plans to do. If she simply wants to be heard, you may be able to maneuver her out of the public eye and into a space where you can talk privately. If, however, her goal is to embarrass you and your establishment, it may be time to call security—or even the police. You may not need to complete the call: When the customer sees you take out your phone and dial 911, she may realize she could find herself in jail overnight, which may be enough to send her on her way—or at least lower the volume.

INVITATION TO A FIGHT

A customer who actually threatens violence may or may not be serious. If you see no weapon, but the customer looks like he might take a swing at you, take a step backward and raise your hands to your sides, palms out, so he can see that you are not making fists. Say out loud, "I'm not going to fight you, sir." When he sees that he cannot bait you, he may back down right away. If he continues to come toward you, however, keep your head and your cool. This can be a frightening situation at best and a dangerous one at worst, so don't be the one to escalate it into a fistfight (which, by the way, will almost certainly get you fired). Instead, call for reinforcements from your coworkers. Repeat in a louder voice, "I'm not going to fight you, sir," and then add, "but I'm sure someone here has already called 911." If they haven't, they should. Again, the threat of police involvement will be enough to make most people back down.

A MOUTHFUL OF PROFANITY

A customer who swears at you is rarely angry with you personally, even if she says something to the effect of, "You are a f***ing
a**hole." In most cases, she knows nothing about you, apart
from her inaccurate perception that you're standing between
her and her desired resolution to her problem. Once you know
this, the actual words she uses become far less painful.

Do your best not to become defensive when a customer
chooses to use profanity. Ignore the actual words and continue
smoothly with the conversation. Say to her, "Ma'am, I really do
want to help. What will it take to solve this successfully for you?"
This may disarm her enough that you can go on from there, especially if she gives you a reasonable alternative. If she doesn't, you
can say, "I wish I could do that, ma'am, but I can't; however, I can
do this." And then make your best offer. Your attempt to meet her
halfway may neutralize her outburst even further.

WHEN THE SWEARING IS INDEED DIRECTED AT YOU

Let's say you're a fast food worker and you accidentally put
a serving of French fries on the same tray as a customer's ice
cream. He didn't order the fries, and is suddenly ranting at you
in abusive language. (This actually happened at a McDonald's in
Ypsilanti, Michigan; Google it if you want to be horrified.) What
should you do?

There are situations where there is no way to de-escalate
the conflict. Finish the business as quickly as you can, ideally
without saying anything that will make the situation worse (if
possible, say nothing at all). If you feel threatened, you are well
within your rights to call for security or law enforcement.

"THIS IS BEING RECORDED"

In an age when everything you say and do can be recorded and posted to the Web, it pays to be as polite as possible with every customer. When someone approaches you with a smartphone positioned to take your picture, you can bet something odd is about to happen to you. Take the action as a warning to be on your best behavior, and consider this a great opportunity to demonstrate the finest in customer service.

RACIAL OR ETHNIC SLURS

No one should be allowed to call another human being by a name that slurs her race, religion, or nationality. Still, we know this happens all too frequently. When it happens to you while you're at work, you will most likely want to lash out in kind at the person who insults you.

If only there were a way to do this that would solve the problem for you, and for everyone who shares your skin color or background! The fact is that nothing you do or say will change this person's mind. The most effective thing to do is remove yourself from the situation as quickly and quietly as you can, so you don't have to listen to this abuse. If you work at a store or restaurant counter, chances are your manager will be nearby—and she should come to your aid. If she doesn't step up, ask a coworker to replace you while you excuse yourself from the situation.

If you cannot escape without leaving other customers standing and waiting, do your best to ignore the names this customer calls you, finish the transaction as quickly as you can, and move on to the next person. Your quiet graciousness will impress others at the scene, who are most likely as mortified as you are.

Unreasonable Demands

OUTRAGEOUS REQUESTS

Say your customer in a car dealership feels that the repairs your service department just finished actually damaged his car. You can't see the damage, and your technicians can't figure out what the customer believes he sees. Nevertheless, he demands that you give him a brand new car to make up for the damages.

You have several options in this case, none of which involve actually giving him a new car. You can assure him that your service department will conduct a full evaluation of the vehicle, free of charge, and find the mystery problem and fix it. If he continues to insist that the only proper response is a new car, you can attempt to explain why such a transaction simply isn't possible. You can enlist someone of higher authority—such as the sales manager or (even better) the dealership's owner—to lay out all the realistic alternatives for him. If he still won't relent, your last recourse may be to suggest binding arbitration. This is a distant option, however, and nearly all customers will give in long before you need to go there.

WHEN THE CUSTOMER WON'T LET IT GO

Even the best employees make mistakes occasionally, and chances are you will make one or two in your place of business. You already know to apologize and do what your customer feels is necessary to make things right. Some customers, however, won't let go of the small slight they have experienced at your hands.

If you have done all you can and the problem has been solved, there's nothing to do but let the customer talk until she winds down and walks away. You don't need to respond any more than you already have, so stop talking and try not to become defensive. Eventually this interaction will end.

ENDLESS DEMANDS

Let's say you run an advertising agency, and a client of yours falls into the high-maintenance, low-reward category. This client always wants you to lower your fees, constantly finds fault with your work, insists on many rounds of changes without additional compensation, and then does not pay her bills on time. There's nothing pleasurable about working with her—and she tears apart creative ideas so thoroughly that you can't even point to the quality of your work as worthwhile.

Why are you keeping her? Firing a client is a valid way to do business, especially if the pain of working with her far outweighs the compensation. Finish your current business with her, and then explain that you are going in a different direction. Recommend another firm that she may find appropriate for her needs . . . and walk away. You will find that the space and time this client used to occupy can be better spent prospecting for new clients.

Sarcasm and Threats

"DON'T YOU KNOW WHO I AM?"

Some customers get angry and tell you what's bothering them, while others bring a lifetime's worth of negative experiences and shout them into your face. These customers are not actually reacting to the specific situation; instead, they want to intimidate you into giving them what they want. They don't want to hear that you understand their problem and are willing to work toward a solution. They want you to cower in fear.

Acknowledge such a customer's self-importance, however misguided, and respond to it. Your impulse may be to try to take him down a peg, but as someone committed to a good experience for all, you must take the contention out of the conversation. When he says, "Don't you know who I am? I'm the president of my own company," your best response is, "I did not realize that, sir. Let's see what we can do to get this solved properly for you."

BUT DON'T PATRONIZE

Watch out here, however—there's a fine line between accepting and defusing the customer's strategy, and sounding patronizing. Avoid saying things like, "Oh, my! I didn't realize how important you are." The customer will believe you're making fun of her, and that will be the end of her deeply-buried goodwill.

"I'M GOING TO TELL YOUR MANAGER!"

It's usually a last resort, but a customer may threaten to go over your head and complain about you to management. By all means, let him do so. If you know that you're doing your job, you have nothing to fear. This may even be a good time to ask your manager, "What could I have done differently? I'd like to learn from this."

Oblige the customer who wants to complain to a higher authority. "Certainly, you're welcome to speak with her. Her name is Cynthia Rodriguez, and you can reach her at 555-3456. Would you like her e-mail address?" Then let your manager know she's about to hear from this customer, and give her some background from your perspective.

"I'M GOING TO PUT YOU OUT OF BUSINESS!"

Single-handedly? It's unlikely that any one customer's complaint will achieve this, unless your product actually killed someone (and even this does not close down companies these days—just ask Toyota and Ford). When he threatens to call the Better Business Bureau, plaster his story all over the Internet, or call in the crack investigative team at the local TV news station, acknowledge his right to do so. "Of course, you can speak to whomever you like. I would genuinely like you to be happy with your purchase, though, so let's see what we can do for you."

"I'M GOING TO SUE!"

People who are actually going to engage an attorney and file a lawsuit rarely proclaim this in the middle of a store. Respond to such a threat by acknowledging the anger, and once again offer to resolve the issue. "I understand how this has upset you. Honestly, I want to help find the best solution for you. Here are the options I can offer."

"YOU'RE SUCH A CONTROL FREAK!"

You're following company policy, but your customer doesn't like it. The insult (if you see it as one) is harmless, so treat it as such. Say, "I understand how you feel, but I am careful to follow the rules of this company. I am very sorry that I can't do what you want me to."

"I'LL GO TO YOUR COMPETITION!"

Let's say you work for a cable company, and your customer feels your rates are too high. She may threaten to dump her cable service and go to satellite TV. Your company wants you to list all the benefits and advantages of staying with cable, but you will be better served by working to solve the customer's issues. Say, "I know it's hard to see your bill come every month, but you are getting a lot of good services that you won't get with satellite TV. I can review them all with you, if you would like to have a clearer understanding of what you're paying for."

"I WANT A NEW CUSTOMER DISCOUNT!"

Small business owners hear this a lot, and some capitulate and give the new customer a discount just to get his business. The trouble with this, of course, is that you can never reverse the discount and get full price from him. You are locked into a situation in which you are not making money, but you are giving him the best of your services.

This customer doesn't care that lowering your price for him could be detrimental to your business, so there's no point in trying to explain that. Instead of giving in, ask him to see reason. "I'm sure some companies do this, and you are an important customer to us. But please understand that we consider all our customers to be equally important to our business, so our pricing is the same for everyone."

"I DON'T DEAL WITH PEOPLE LIKE YOU"

You may encounter the self-important customer who does not want to deal with an "underling"—someone who only wants the attention of the owner. Running to fetch the owner is rarely practical, though, and chances are he expects you to handle people like this anyway. Smile and say, "I can look for the owner for you, but that may take some time. I can also save you the time by helping you with what you need. You said you're looking for a new watch. Do you have a particular style or price range in mind?" Continuing with the transaction will gain you some respect from the customer, and the rest will hopefully proceed without additional incident.

"I'M GOING TO CALL THE MEDIA!"

A dissatisfied customer threatens to call every travel journalist in the world if she doesn't get the discount she wants on her hotel room. And she might—though they are very unlikely to take the bait, and few will even acknowledge the correspondence. The likelihood that this threat is thin, however, doesn't change the fact that you have an angry customer in front of you. Smile and say, "Of course, you have a right to talk with the media and anyone else you like, and I would not dream of stopping you. I am very sorry that I can't help you with the discount. Is there any other way I can make your stay more enjoyable?"

"I'M NOT GOING TO PAY!"

You're an independent contractor, and you've just finished work on your customer's new bathroom. It looks wonderful to you, but the customer now decides he hates the countertops. He wants you to replace them with something else, "and I won't pay a dime until you do."

You've done exactly what he ordered and you know you're not at fault, but saying so will not help you. Instead, say, "Wow, you're really disappointed with the countertops. Tell me more about why you don't like them." Gain a good understanding of the problem, and then offer solutions: "Let me bring in some samples and you can choose something else right here, so you can see the colors in relation to the rest of the room." Then, make it clear that there will be a charge for the change. "I am very sorry that you are not happy with the countertops. The cost of replacing them with this new material will be $800." If you have been reasonable and helpful throughout this crisis, you should be able to negotiate a fair price with the customer.

"BUT WHY?"

Sometimes you will encounter people who have had training in asserting their opinions, or even in intimidating others. Many have life coaches or take self-help classes that promise to boost their confidence. Unfortunately, some of these also promote self-assertion at the expense of others.

One common result is that this type of customer will keep asking "why?" until he backs you into a verbal corner, from which your only escape seems to be to grant his demand. But you don't have to succumb to this. Here's how such a conversation might go.

> **You:** "I'm sorry, but it's company policy not to take back merchandise that was purchased on clearance."
>
> **Customer:** "But why?"
>
> **You:** "This merchandise is priced to sell at the end of a season, so it's sold at a very deep discount. The understanding is that you're getting a bargain, so there is no return."
>
> **Customer:** "But why?"
>
> **You:** "We actually have nowhere to stock end-of-season merchandise. After the sale ends, we have no way to sell it. That's why it's so deeply discounted."
>
> **Customer:** "But why?"

The customer thinks he has you, but you can prove him wrong and end this cycle.

> **You:** "Sir, I understand you are dissatisfied with this item. Can you tell me what you didn't like about it?"

Now he has to answer you, or appear rude. You may still have a difficult customer on your hands, but at least you have ended the stream of whys.

"YOUR PRODUCT MESSED UP MY HOUSE"

You're carrying a new product, and when the customer used it at home, it damaged her floors. Obviously, you'll take the product back and refund her money, but she also wants you to pay to fix her floors.

This is a problem for the manufacturer, so gently steer the customer in that direction. "Wow, I am so sorry that you had this trouble with this new product. I'm sure the manufacturer will want to know exactly what happened, and they will probably want to deal with you directly. Let me make the first contact for you, and then I'll turn them over to you so they can make this right. I really want to know how this turns out, so I'll follow up with you in a few days. Thank you so much for bringing this to my attention."

The Fibbing Customer

THE ACCIDENTAL LIE

Most customers do not mean to lie, but if you work in customer service, you are sure to encounter some who do. It's your job to anticipate various kinds of untruths and do your best to seek the real story behind them.

Suppose you work for a company that sells laundry detergent. A customer calls and says your blue-colored detergent has stained her white socks. There's no way this can happen—the detergent dissolves in water—but the customer believes it did. You are happy to offer her coupons for other purchases, of course, but part of you wonders if she's fishing for them.

You say, "Wow, that must have really made you angry, having your white clothes ruined like that. It's funny, but we've never had this complaint before. I'd like to know more about what happened. Can you tell me what else was in the load of laundry?"

By probing gently, you discover there was a drawstring laundry bag in the load, and the drawstring is made of blue rope. You suggest, "I don't want to rule out the detergent, but that cord may have been what stained your socks. Let me send you a coupon for a free bottle of detergent, for your trouble. I also have some tips for getting dye stains out of white clothing. Would you like to hear them?" No one is offended, and the customer gets something for free and some help for her problem.

FREE LUNCH

A client of your law firm e-mails you and says he needs your services. He asks if you can meet for lunch at a restaurant he enjoys. You say yes, of course, knowing that you will pick up the tab, and you bring two other attorneys who can handle the kind of work you usually get from him. When you arrive at the restaurant and are seated, however, he tells you that it turns out he doesn't need your services after all. Now three expensive attorneys are just sitting there instead of billing their time, and your client's getting a free lunch. You suspect he lied to get it.

What do you do? Nothing at all. There's nothing to do but smile, enjoy the lunch, and excuse yourself as soon as you can to get back to work. This is a "fool me once, shame on you" kind of situation—one that you'll be sure to avoid next time. Before you go, however, ask the client what kind of work he thinks he may have coming up, and how your firm may help.

"ARE YOU NEW HERE?"

Maybe you've just started work at a company, but that doesn't mean you can let a customer pull the wool over your eyes. All too often, the question, "Are you new here?" is followed by, "I always get something for free."

Whether you are indeed new or a seasoned veteran at the company, you know a scam when you see it. Smile and say, "Ma'am, you're right, I haven't been with this company for very long. That's why I can't give you that for free without my manager's authorization. Shall I get her for you?" In nearly every case, the customer will back down. She knows you're on to her.

"I CAN GET THIS CHEAPER FROM YOUR COMPETITION"

Your customer may actually believe this, but if you and your company have done your homework, you know exactly what your competition charges for this item—if they carry it at all. If you know for certain, you can say, "Really? The last price I saw on that item at that store was actually a dime more expensive than ours. If you want to bring us an ad or a photo with a time and date stamp, however, we would be happy to match the price."

"THE CHECK IS IN THE MAIL"

Maybe it is and maybe it isn't, but if you're a small business owner and you don't receive payment a few days after you're told you will, you are in a tough position. It can be galling to explain this to a customer who has already received your services—but the National Foundation for Credit Counseling tells us one-third of all consumers don't pay their bills on time.

What do you do? If the check doesn't come, send a polite letter to the customer with an invoice marked "past due." Then follow up by phone, and calmly explain to him that any additional work will have to be put on hold until the payment arrives. If he has an urgent need for more work from you, he is likely to pay. If he tries to beg off payment but still needs the work, stop working for him. Otherwise, you'll just be using up more time for which you won't get paid.

THE USED RETURN

A customer purchases a pair of gloves online from your company. A week after she receives them, you get them back in the mail. They are no longer in their original package, and it's clear that they have been worn at least once: The fingers are dirty on the right-hand glove. Your company has a strict policy—written on your shipping statement and on your website—that returns must be in new condition and in their original packaging in order to be valid.

Do you refund the customer's money? She knows she's returning used goods. Send her an e-mail stating that the gloves were not returned in their original packaging, and restate your company policy. It's good to write a series of standard e-mails that are ready to send out in cases such as this. If the customer gives you trouble, it's up to you to decide whether you want to give her a refund. A protracted haggle over a $20 pair of gloves may not be worth your time.

Something Isn't Right

CUSTOMER IN DISTRESS

Many complaints about inappropriate reactions to urgent situations come from hospital emergency rooms—in fact, they come up so frequently that they have become fodder for situation comedies and stand-up routines. Patients in distress all too often encounter desk personnel who demand that they fill out reams of paperwork before a doctor will see them. When this happens to a woman in labor or a person with severe chest pain, the situation becomes dangerous.

Wherever you work, if a customer approaches you and speaks in a loud voice, listen to what he's saying before jumping to the conclusion that he is yelling at you in anger. He may be having a heart attack, suffering from an injury, or panicking over something he can see and you can't. You should react to the emergency in progress, not to breaches of company procedure.

GET THERE FIRST

You work in a car wash, and a customer who has just gone through the line drives her car back to the entrance again. You take a quick glance and see that the thick coating of dead bugs on her front bumper did not come off the first time through. Defuse the anger as soon as she drives up: "Hey, ma'am, I see all those bugs didn't come off. Go ahead and drive through again." Your customer has no need to be angry, and may even nod and smile at you as she proceeds into the tunnel for another wash.

MISSING PARTS

When a customer calls to say that the order he just received has missing parts, the call should be fairly routine: an apology from the customer service rep and a shipment of these parts. This can escalate to crisis level, however, if the manufacturer insists that its quality control processes are so infallible that it's actually impossible for any parts to be missing. If you happen to work for a company that believes itself to be watertight, take the customer at his word and send out the parts—and then share this information with your manager. There are plenty of stories on the Web about the number of times the "infallible process" has failed, and customers have had to wrangle missing parts out of companies that insisted they could not be missing.

THE RUDE COWORKER

You own a retail store, and one of your employees pulls you over to deal with an angry customer. The customer immediately turns to you and says, "This clerk was very rude to me!"

No doubt she would love to see you berate this employee, but that would not be the best response. Instead, say, "I'm terribly sorry. Of course, you deserve to be treated well in our store. Tell me what was said, and I will deal with this employee privately."

When you've heard the story, make sure she gets what she needs. "Thank you so much for telling me about this. Now, have you found what you were looking for? Can I help you complete your purchase?"

STORM IN THE CALL CENTER

When the company you work for has a major problem—a power outage, for example—you're going to find yourself deluged with calls from angry customers. This is a great day to learn how to shield your personal feelings from criticism and abuse. Begin each call by listening to the customer, and then apologize on behalf of the company for his inconvenience. If you can't yet provide timelines for repairs or restoration of power, tell him, "I can assure you that the company is aware of the problem, and that they are working on a timeline to get everyone back up and running. We do know how great an inconvenience this is; we are doing everything we can to collect more information on the issue and share it with you." If possible, find out where else people can go for this information as it becomes available, so you don't get triple the calls you can handle.

THE ALLERGIC REACTION

You work in a restaurant, and a customer at one of your tables suddenly grabs her throat with one hand and reaches into a pocket with another. She pulls out an EpiPen and jabs herself in the thigh with it. Meanwhile, her husband begins yelling at the top of his lungs, "Are there *peanuts* in this food?"

The customer never mentioned a peanut allergy, but it makes no difference in the midst of a medical emergency. Go to the table immediately and find out if someone has called 911, or if you need to do so. Take away the plate in front of the afflicted patron, and ask if there is anything else you can do to help. Chances are the family will know exactly what needs to be done. Don't get defensive, especially if no one is pointing a finger at you in accusation. Your concern must be for the woman with the medical condition.

THE BAD NEWS

Call center employees often find themselves being the bearers of bad news to people they have never met. For example, customer service reps at health insurance companies regularly tell people that they are not covered for a medical procedure they desperately need. The response, of course, is most often anger—all of it directed at the person who delivered the news, when it's really meant for the company.

If you are in this situation, you can defuse the worst of the anger by paraphrasing what the customer says to you. When he says, "This is absolutely unfair, and you should be ashamed that I can't get this procedure," it's your turn to say, "You really need this procedure, and it's not fair that you aren't covered for it." You are commiserating instead of acting as the adversary, and while you can't offer him coverage for his medical problem, you can at least calm him down.

What Not to Do

SHOULDA, WOULDA, COULDA

The last thing a customer wants to hear from you or any other employee of your company is, "Well, you should have done it this way." When a customer comes to you with unfinished paperwork, an expired warranty, a broken product, or an overdue bill, he wants solutions to his problem, not admonishments for doing something incorrectly. Instead of scolding him, try this: "These forms are all so complicated, aren't they? Let's go through this one and see if we can get all the questions answered," or, "While your item is out of warranty, there may still be something we can do to help you get the service you need."

DON'T BE A SCHOOLMARM

You work at the Department of Motor Vehicles, and a customer comes up to you with questions about filling out a complex form. There might be some environments in which you could play the taskmistress and tsk-tsk-tsk at her for not following all of your department's procedures . . . but a customer service situation is never the place for that. You will have more success if you say: "Could you give me all the papers you've brought with you? Let me check these over and make sure you have everything before you spend time standing in line." Your helpful demeanor will get you much further with customers, especially those who see your department as a necessary evil.

THE CRISIS OF YOUR OWN MAKING

You run a home renovation business, and you've been working on a customer's kitchen. You've reached the point in the process where he begins to install all the electrical lines himself, as planned. He's moving slowly and putting you behind schedule. As another day goes by and he hasn't called to tell you he's finished the job, you reach for the phone to berate him.

How do you think this is going to go? As far as the customer is concerned, you are creating a crisis—not he. He's enjoying the process and saving himself some money, and he's simply not as fast as your usual electrical contractor. He knows you were informed from the beginning that he was going to do his own electrical work, so you should have made enough time in your schedule for this. If you didn't, that's your fault, not his.

If you must call, do so in a friendly way. Say, "Hey, I'm just checking in to see if you've got everything you need on the electrical end. I want to plan the next phase of the project and keep it on schedule for your family, so could you give me an idea of when I should bring in the drywall crew?" It's his name on the check, not yours. You may find he doesn't want to hold you up any more than you want him to delay you.

TELLING THE CUSTOMER WHAT TO DO

Why did that customer just turn her back on you and storm out of your store? Perhaps it was the way you said to her, "Get over there to the end of the line, ma'am," when you found her standing between two lines of customers waiting to check out. A better way to handle that situation would be to ask her, "Ma'am, did you mean to be in line?" and see if she needs your help or direction. Barking orders will never earn you repeat customers.

ILLEGAL REQUESTS

Hotel employees are most likely to get customer requests for something that not only compromises their principles, but may also be against the law. Requests for illicit drugs or prostitutes can make them wonder if they are expected to do whatever it takes to make a customer happy, even if it could land them in jail. The answer to this is a resounding "No." If a guest approaches you with a request that crosses the line, however, there's no need to embarrass her with a horrified response. Simply say, "I'm sorry, ma'am, I wouldn't have any idea how to get that," and extricate yourself from the conversation as quickly and graciously as you can.

DANGEROUS REQUESTS

Your guest's request may not be illegal, but if it puts you or him in some kind of danger, you may be very uncomfortable granting it. If, for example, he asks you to turn up the temperature of the hot water heater in his room to a degree that could result in a serious burn, you would be well within your rights to decline. "I understand that you'd like a higher temperature," you could respond, "but we are only insured for the maximum temperature the hot water heaters reach now. It's company policy, and I have to support it."

It Gets Worse

WHEN THE CUSTOMER IS DRUNK

You work in a restaurant with a bar, and a customer has had several drinks too many. She's being sloppy, loud, and irritating to other customers. Cutting her off is the easy part—now you need to find a way to get her home safely, even if she did most of her drinking at another establishment. Call a cab, walk her to the door, and make sure she gets into the vehicle. Most drunken people will not try to attack you, but they may try to refuse to get into a taxi. Enlist the help of one or more other staff members if it looks like they may become unruly.

DEALING WITH A BODY

You're a front desk clerk at a small hotel, and you get a call to come to a guest's room right away for an emergency. When you arrive, you find a nearly hysterical wife and a dead husband. Your customer service skills come into play in the way you deal with the living, and how quickly and quietly you can get this emergency under control. Remember that you have a (probably) grieving widow demanding your attention, but also many practical concerns such as how to deal with the body and keep other guests from becoming curious onlookers. Ask the wife if you can call other family members for her, wait for the police and ambulance with her, or help her make or change travel arrangements. Help her stay out of the way of gawkers and guests who are already whispering as they pass her in the hall. Finally, comp the cost of the room.

THE SENSITIVE ISSUE

Sometimes the best thing you can offer a customer is quiet discretion. For example, if he comes into your pharmacy and wants to discuss which ointment will be most effective for his hemorrhoids, he certainly doesn't want to do it in the middle of the aisle with other customers jostling their way past him. Be alert to the signs that a customer needs to speak with you privately, and give him the opportunity to take you aside. Remember to keep your voice down, as well.

THE PUBLIC RELATIONS NIGHTMARE

Before you go into work one morning, you hear on the national news that your employer has decided to take a stand on an issue that has nothing to do with his business or products. The stand is controversial at best and bigoted at worst. You have to be at work in an hour, and you know you're going to be approached all day by customers who are either delighted or deeply offended by the statement.

Take a few minutes to look up the telephone number and e-mail address of the corporate headquarters, and make yourself a sheet of contact information that you can hand to customers who want to make themselves heard. When they or other protesters approach you, simply say, "I'm as surprised as you are. Here's where you can contact the management of the company to tell them what you think." No matter how you yourself feel about the news, don't commiserate or rejoice with customers. The more contentious the issue, the worse it will be if someone overhears your personal opinion while you're talking with someone else.

Customer Service in a Real-Life Crisis

THE AUTOMOBILE DEFECT

When a pedal defect made many of its cars accelerate without warning, possibly resulting in the deaths of 34 people, Toyota recalled 2.3 million vehicles—but another week went by before it issued an apology to those who had been harmed. Getting the cars off the road as quickly as possible was the right thing to do, but waiting to make a public statement to customers was a mistake as big as the initial defect. Toyota lost $21 billion in market value from the combined impact of this recall and its reluctance to show public concern for its injured clients.

OWNING THE MISTAKE, CONTROLLING THE MESSAGE

When the social media publishing app Buffer suffered a security breach that caused thousands of spam messages to appear on Facebook, the company opted for total transparency in its response. Buffer's team immediately posted the problem on Twitter with an apology for the breach and the service outage. The company also blogged throughout the day about the ways in which it was working to get service back online. Within hours, the problem had been solved, and customers knew how to get back into their accounts. The company received praise from online media, and retained its customer base with barely a hiccup.

FAT-SHAMING ENDS IN AIRLINE SHAME

Who knows what regulation the captain of a Southwest Airlines flight felt he was following when he ordered Kevin Smith off his plane, telling him he was "too fat to fly." Smith had unusual talents at his fingertips, however—not only did he have a smartphone, but, as a film director, he also knew how to create dramatic tension. He took to Twitter, describing the entire incident and including @SouthwestAir in his tweets. To its credit, the company responded immediately with apologies on its website and in its own Twitter feed, but this did not keep the incident from being reported by *USA Today* and ABC News. (See more about the speed and power of social media in Part Seven.)

TERRORISTS AT THE TAJ MUMBAI

When terrorist gunshots were heard inside the Taj Mahal Palace Hotel in Mumbai, India, in November 2008, the 24-year-old banquet manager calmly took over the protection of the guests at a party in the second floor banquet room. He and about 25 other employees instructed the guests to get down under the tables and stay quiet, and they all waited in silence as the terrorists detonated grenades and shot down hotel guests outside the room. There they stayed until morning, when the staff asked the guests to move to the windows and wave down to the firefighters outside. They were spotted right away and rescued, and no one in the room was injured—though 52 people in other parts of the hotel, most of them employees, were killed or wounded in the attack. The employees were well trained, resourceful, and courteous to the guests throughout the crisis, and a number of them formed human shields to protect guests during the evacuation.

THE SONY STORM

More than 77 million customers were affected when the Sony PlayStation Network got hacked in 2011, but most of them didn't know how badly they might have been compromised until days later. Sony recognized the attack and shut down the network on April 20, but it took the company another six days to admit it "couldn't rule out the possibility" that customers' personal information, including their credit card data, had fallen into the hands of the hackers. Amid outrage over the next several days, Sony offered all users a free year of identity theft protection. Two weeks later, with criticism still pouring in, it offered its users in most parts of the world their choice of several PlayStation 3 and PSP games. It took the company even longer to offer choices to players in Asia.

THE UNFEELING CABLE COMPANY

Some residents of Alabama lost their homes and all of their possessions in tornadoes in 2011, but they received no sympathy from Charter Cable. According to whistle-blower website Stop The Cap!, they were told they had to pay for cable boxes lost during the storms. Website reporters actually recorded Charter customer service reps telling customers, "If your house was destroyed, and you have looked around the neighborhood for our cable box and cannot find it, you owe us $212 and you need to either pay us or make an insurance claim on our behalf." Once the media began to carry the story, it set off a public outcry that made Charter "adjust" the policy, crediting affected customers for their equipment and no longer requesting that they needed to file a claim for the loss with their homeowners' insurance.

THE AIRLINE BAGGAGE FAIL

Remember back in Part One, when you learned about the lute player who flew Delta Airlines and found his priceless instrument smashed to pieces? United Airlines made the same mistake with Dave Carroll, lead singer and guitar player in Canadian folk duo Sons of Maxwell. Carroll wrote a song about the incident, turned it into a catchy music video, and posted it on YouTube. Business Insider.com reports that the backlash from the song's 10 million views forced United to reimburse the musician for the $1,200 he'd spent to repair his guitar. The airline had been stonewalling his request for weeks. The song, "United Breaks Guitars," made Carroll an Internet sensation and dramatically improved his career. United, however, suffered a 10 percent loss in market share—estimated at $180 million—on the year following the song's release.

THE PHONE BILL AND
THE DEAD CUSTOMER

How can a company continue to take money from someone who is dead—even after it receives the corresponding death certificate from that person's relatives? That's what Verizon Wireless did to a Florida family until the local watchdog journalists got involved. The phone company kept making withdrawals for bill payments for several months after the family had contacted them, faxed the death certificate, and stopped using the phone. A customer service rep went so far as to laugh at the deceased man's daughter when she called to plead with him to stop charging her father's estate for a closed account. When contacted by the journalists, the company shut down the account and refunded the money back to the date of death. Of course, the story made it into the newspaper and still lives online.

POISON IN THE PILL BOTTLE

Long before the Internet and global call centers, one of the world's most trusted brands faced an epic crisis. A handful of bottles of Tylenol Extra Strength, the over-the-counter pain reliever, were found to contain cyanide. The poison killed seven people who took the pills. The company moved swiftly to tell the entire nation to stop using its product. It recalled every bottle from shelves across the country, and refunded customers' money for pills they had purchased.

Johnson & Johnson, makers of Tylenol, established a toll-free number for questions about the crisis. This allowed customer service reps to respond to frightened customers with compassion and reassurance. The company then introduced the first tamper-proof packaging, a model for the packaging we see on every over-the-counter medication today. Still one of the most-taught case studies of its kind, this company's fast, sweeping, transparent response and demonstration of concern for its customers enabled it to keep its image as a trusted brand.

THE INCORRECT PRESCRIPTION

After filling a customer's prescription incorrectly for nearly a year, giving her 10 times her doctor's prescribed dosage, Walgreens stopped returning her calls for compensation—even after she started missing work and had to have surgery to relieve the pain the hiked dosage had caused her. After she took her case to the media, Walgreens was forced to provide a better response. The company issued an apology on ABC News, and said they "will work to prevent this type of incident from happening in the future." The patient also received an apology, though it's not clear if she was compensated for the medical expenses and loss of work.

THE BANK WE LOVE TO HATE

When customer Ann Minch discovered that Bank of America had hiked her credit card interest rate from 13 percent to 30 percent, she launched a "Debtors' Revolt" on YouTube with a video calling the high interest rate "usury and plundering," and calling out the bank at which she had been a customer for 14 years with nary a late payment. "I could get a better rate from a loan shark," she said. "I did call Bank of America, and they weren't willing to negotiate anything." In two weeks, Minch had appeared on national television and her video had gone viral on many websites. Bank of America agreed to lower her interest rate.

POWER OUTAGE: NOT THE POWER COMPANY'S FAULT

When a major ice storm took out power to most of a midsize city in upstate New York, the power company received thousands of calls from customers' cellular phones; in fact, these quickly overloaded the utility's communications system. Management understood the need to give customers as much information as possible on when their power might be restored, what progress had been made in their specific area, and where to go for emergency shelter if their homes got too cold or there were people with special medical needs living with them. Customer service reps received timely updates so they could keep people informed and let them know if it was time to move to a warmer place. Rather than conveying the stress they must have felt, the people staffing the phones carried an important, calming message to those shivering at home: "You are not alone. We know you are there, and we are all in this together."

POWER OUTAGE: THE POWER COMPANY'S FAULT

"Rolling blackouts" seemed to be the only way to maintain power in California during a particularly shaky time in 2000 and 2001. Customers received a number on their electric bills telling them what power grid they were getting their electricity from. This was the only indication they had about when their power might be shut off, often for as long as two and a half hours, to allow other grids to operate.

While the best customer service option in such a situation would be to get power to everyone (as the state finally did), the power industry learned some valuable lessons about communicating with customers. One of the most important was this: Customers are more angry when the power outage is the power company's fault than they are if the problem is the result of a natural disaster or other outside cause. In this case, the problem stemmed from market manipulation—and customer service representatives had the personal choice of repeating corporate excuses to callers or commiserating with their anger over skyrocketing electricity bills. We can only guess that many of them chose the latter (probably reducing some users' anger).

PART

6

BUILDING CUSTOMER LOYALTY

How do you keep customers coming back again and again? Making them feel valued, important, and appreciated is only the first part of the customer loyalty equation. The rest involves making your company or organization stand out from the rest by delivering the kind of customer service that goes the extra mile.

How do you go the extra mile? In this part, you'll learn how following up with your customers affirms their value to you, while also helping you keep your promises to them. At the end of this part you'll find some legendary stories from the world of customer service, including how companies like the Ritz Carlton, Apple, and Southwest Airlines became the power-houses of customer loyalty they are today—true examples of how to turn first-time customers into lifelong fans. You may have heard some of these stories before, but with all of them together in one place, you'll be able to detect some interesting patterns. Each of these stories presents an exciting surprise or an unusual problem, and a diligent, caring, often innovative way of solving it. What can your company learn from these tales of highly considerate, over-the-top service? Before you get to that, you'll explore the day-to-day difference you can make in the lives of your customers, cementing your relationship through small gestures that will keep them coming back.

All of this adds up to a better bottom line, through a repeat clientele who talk to their friends, families, coworkers, and the world at large about the things you do to make them feel special.

Invest in Your People

SHARE STORIES INTERNALLY

At staff meetings, have employees share stories of customer interactions they've had in the past week, and discuss what everyone can learn from each of them. Do this without judgment, encouraging all of your employees to participate openly. Have them volunteer ideas about how a conversation could have gone better, or what this one employee did that was really admirable. Soon they will see that you've created a safe environment for learning, and that you value their ability to provide the best in customer service.

EMULATE THE RIGHT EXAMPLES

Do your customers have half an hour to wait in a call queue for an answer to a simple question? When someone finally answers the phone, does she start the session by quizzing the customer on his address, phone number, e-mail address, and other information that is not relevant to his question? If so, your call center may be operating based on what you need, rather than what the customer needs. He doesn't have time to sit and wait, and then be frustrated by a rep who seems unwilling to listen.

Think carefully about what you hate about other companies' call centers or customer service lines, and make sure *none of that* takes place at yours. Take those miserable examples as the cautionary tales they are, and build a new call center approach based on your core philosophy of excellent customer service.

DEVELOP A SERVICE CULTURE

You're talking the talk, but are you walking the walk? If you want your employees to make customer service a top priority, you need to practice what you preach. Demonstrate the kind of customer relationships you want to see from your employees by building these relationships yourself. Formalize the steps you want your employees to take to please customers, turning these into a document to which they can refer. This means more than hanging up signs that repeat old platitudes about how "the customer is always right"—it is an articulation of the philosophy by which you run your company.

For example, the global theater rigging company J.R. Clancy has at the core of its corporate culture the slogan, "Make our partners successful." The company commits to delivering every order "on time, complete, and correct," and listens carefully to its customers when it makes design decisions for new products. The result is that clients receive what they need the first time around—and the rigging is designed to be easy to install, taking into account the kinds of challenges people encounter when putting a new rigging system into a theater. This level of customer service is central to the company's entire culture, from design to engineering to sales.

GET EVERYONE ON THE SAME PAGE

If you're a business owner, you need to set expectations for your employees about what kind of customer service you want them to offer. Teach them the skills they need to give your customers that standout level of service. Only a handful of potential hires will come to you with these skills and insights already in place; it's up to you to bring everyone else up to speed, and to make service commitment part of your company's culture.

EXCELLENT SERVICE IS EVERYONE'S JOB

Every employee on your staff needs to have the same training in customer service. If you make it the job of only one department, you are almost certain to discover that a customer stopped patronizing your business because an employee in a different department—one you didn't believe had much interaction with customers—behaved in a way that was completely counter to the culture you've worked to create. From the front desk staff to the bean counters in the back office, everyone must know what you expect of them whenever they talk with, text, or e-mail a customer.

TREAT YOUR EMPLOYEES LIKE CUSTOMERS

Adrian Miller writes on the Business Knowhow website that customer service reps "carry around within them a little algebraic equation. It goes like this: If you treat *me* badly, and expect me to treat customers *well*, then this equation will not reconcile. There will be a discrepancy. That discrepancy, in human customer service terms, is *hypocrisy*." Make no mistake—your employees can spot insincerity at 50 paces. Demonstrate the behavior you want them to embrace, especially in your interactions with them. Listen to what they have to say, give them respect and courtesy, and work to resolve any issues in the fairest possible way. This is the way you want them to treat customers. If you treat them the same way, they will believe you mean what you say.

GIVE YOUR EMPLOYEES
THE TOOLS THEY NEED

Employees need a clear idea of what they can promise to do for customers and where they must draw the line. Build a hierarchy of things they can do to correct an error: compensate with an alternative offer, take back an item after the cutoff date, or give a credit or refund, for instance. Make this information available to all staff members dealing with customers, and review changes with them regularly so they understand what tools they have at their disposal. If you empower them to make their own judgment calls, you will see more issues resolved more quickly—which will make your customers happier.

GIVE EMPLOYEES THE TIME THEY NEED
TO RESOLVE AN ISSUE

It's not uncommon for customer service or call center employees to have a time limit within which they must close an issue. Few things are more infuriating to customers than the sense that they're being rushed, especially if they've waited a long time in line or on hold to talk to you. Companies that throw out the time limit generally find that their clients are more satisfied with the service experience, and more issues are resolved in the first contact. In fact, according to a study by Lee Resources, 70 percent of complaining customers will continue to do business with you if you resolve their complaint, while 95 percent will continue if you resolve it during their first contact with you. The more flexible your employees can be with their time, the more customers will receive the help they need.

Make a Connection

REMEMBER NAMES

It's just about the simplest thing you can do: Recognize a repeat customer and greet her by her name. If you struggle to remember it, choose something about her that you can associate with it—a rhyme, or a word that starts with the same letter. "Randy the redhead," "Nancy who isn't fancy," or "Bill from Brighton" are all easy to remember. Find the right mnemonic device for each of your regular customers.

BE PLEASANT AND PERSONABLE

Your customers are people, just like you, and they enjoy dealing with pleasant people who are willing to chat and get to know them. Smile, make eye contact, compliment them on a striking piece of jewelry or a nice tie, and make a connection that goes beyond asking for a credit card. If you're ringing up a customer's purchase, note what he has selected and ask a question: "Have you bought this before? I've been thinking about it and I wonder how it works." If it's a clothing purchase, compliment him on the color he chose or note that you've had your eye on that sweater as well. Even if the customer approached you with a scowl and a crease of impatience across his forehead, he will leave with a smile and a slightly lighter cloud over his day.

REMEMBER DRINK ORDERS

Do you have a favorite restaurant for Sunday morning brunch?
If you go to the same place every weekend, chances are your
server will suddenly appear at your table with your drink order
before you even ask. Local diner servers are some of the best at
making customers feel welcome and special. You may not serve
beverages in your job, but you may know other things about
your customers' preferences, including what they last purchased. Saying to a returning customer, "Are you back for the
earrings to go with that necklace?" will bring a smile to her face.

NOTICE DETAILS

Let's say you're an accountant and you're meeting with a new
client in his office. As you sit down, you glance around and
notice that there's a model of Doctor Who's TARDIS time
machine on her desk. You sit down and ask, "So, who's your
favorite Doctor?" In seconds you're talking about the merits
of Tom Baker versus David Tennant, and you've struck up an
immediate rapport with her.

Instead of staring at your computer screen or your register
as a customer approaches you, look at her and see what you
can learn about her. Is there a lapel pin that gives you a clue?
Is she wearing a T-shirt with her university logo or her favorite
band? If you're meeting in her environment, take a look around
for things you may have in common. Anything from photos
on the desk to small items on a bookshelf can trigger a great
conversation that will help you build a connection beyond
the task at hand.

LEARN WHAT THEY LIKE

In the hospitality industry, it's critical to know what your repeat customers like: their preferred size of hotel room or bed, whether they smoke or not, whether they travel with pets, and—in the very best hotels—even what they want stocked in their minibar. It's easy to keep track of that kind of information these days, and front desk staff should have access to it whenever a repeat guest makes a reservation. If you can say to him, "Mr. Jones, last time you were here you had dinner in our main restaurant. I'd be happy to make a reservation for your first night here," you will have built a bond with him. He will tell his associates, "I always stay at the Grand Hotel, because they know exactly what I like."

THINK ABOUT THEM WHEN THEY'RE NOT THINKING ABOUT YOU

Now that online systems enable many kinds of vendors to send e-mail receipts to customers for their transactions, your company can collect e-mail addresses as a matter of course. Instead of sending out a generic newsletter to all of your customers, take a little more time to send specific people news of sales on merchandise you know they like. If you can send a short personal note with the information—"Hi Cindy, I saw this was on sale and thought you'd want to know! All the best, Tara"—you will let your customer know that you thought about her when you didn't have to. This kind of service can spark a great deal of repeat business.

KEEP EXCELLENT RECORDS

Here's an enviable scenario: A customer comes into her favorite clothing store looking for a matching accessory to go with an outfit she bought a year ago. She doesn't have the outfit on or with her, however, so she's not sure which handbag will be the right color. A salesperson approaches her, and she explains her predicament. To her surprise, the salesperson says, "Let's just check our records and see what you purchased, and then we can make a perfect match." He then goes to the computer and pulls up the customer's name and a list of every purchase she has made there in the past five years. "Okay," he says, "you need the darker blue bag." The customer is happy that she won't have to make another trip to this store to bring the outfit with her, and she buys the bag as well as a matching necklace and earrings.

Any store can do this today, and many of them do. Even if you run an independent boutique, you can create this kind of system and delight your customers with your knowledge of what they've purchased and what they like.

Make the Effort to Help

"DID YOU FIND EVERYTHING YOU WERE LOOKING FOR?"

In every Wegmans supermarket in the country, employees at the registers begin their transactions with customers by asking, "Did you find everything you were looking for?" If the answer is no, they immediately ask what's missing—and if the item is in the store, they send a runner to get it for you. Not only does Wegmans increase revenue with this strategy, but it also makes its customers feel as if they never need to go elsewhere for a grocery item. (We'll talk more about Wegmans later in this part.)

"HOW CAN I HELP YOU TODAY?"

Some stores have floorwalkers who are well aware of you and will come to your aid if you need it. In other stores, you can't find a soul around when you have a question. There's a delicate balance between leaving customers alone to shop and steering them to a sale, but the best stores know exactly what to do. Here's a simple guideline: Let the shopper decide how much attention he would like. Ask, "How can I help you today?" to let him know that you're available and ready to direct him. Answer any question he may have, and be nearby and ready to help if he needs you to—but don't lurk around like a vulture. Customers appreciate attention when they want it, but they also need a certain degree of privacy to make their own decisions.

KNOW YOUR BUSINESS AND INVENTORY

Whether you work for an auto dealership, a clothing store, or a railroad locomotive manufacturer, you need to be able to answer questions about the products you sell. If you're looking to go the extra mile for your customers, you need to know more than just what's in stock—you should know how the products work, what they do, what they are made of, why some customers prefer certain ones over others, and when you will be ordering more. Make a point of studying your products, so you can answer any question about them that comes your way. A knowledgeable salesperson becomes a valuable company resource, someone the customer will return to again and again for advice and expertise.

Build Trust

MAKE IT EASY

The Customer Contact Council, a division of the Corporate Executive Board, surveyed 75,000 people who had had some interaction with call centers or other customer service departments. They found that the most dependable way to build customer loyalty was to reduce customers' effort in getting their problems solved. The easier you make it for customers, the more likely it is that they will continue to work with your company.

What does it mean to make it easy? Shorter waits on hold, fewer transfers from one department to another, quicker responses from knowledgeable salespeople and customer service reps, simple paths to finding downloads and information on a website: Participants cited all of these as reasons they would continue to patronize one company over another.

DELIVERING ON THE PROMISE

The strongest bonds customers have with brands are built over time, and are based on consistent, dependable delivery of excellent products and service. When you deliver on the promises you make to customers, they learn to trust that you not only build a great product, but that you have their best interests at heart. This kind of trust leads to passion—like the passion Harley-Davidson owners feel for their exceptional motorcycles. Harley, like Apple, has created an experience that transcends the product-buying decision.

DON'T OVERPROMISE

One of the most important ways to build trust is to deliver on what you've promised. That's why it's vital that you do not promise more than you can realistically deliver, or you will set your customer up for a big disappointment. Be as certain as possible about the facts before you inform him of the lengths you can go to please him. Disappointment leads to rejection, while honesty builds trust.

HOW DOES APPLE DO IT?

Here's a startling statistic: According to a study by the Yankee Group, only 9 percent of Apple iPhone users plan to migrate to another platform with their next purchase of a smartphone. In contrast, 24 percent of Android users intend to defect when they get their next phone. Why are Apple users so loyal? It has to do with the total experience of owning an Apple device—the "whole product" we talked about back in Part One. Apple customers buy not only iPhones, but also the leading innovations in smartphone technology, the ever-available support offered at retail Genius Bars, and the knowledge that the company values every single one of its clients. Apple has made it incredibly easy for them to get up and running on a new iPhone: With so many cheerful, diligent employees in every store, shoppers find themselves in the digital queue literally seconds after they've walked in.

Your company probably operates on a much smaller scale, but every business can learn a great deal from the Apple experience. When customers feel valued, cherished, even loved, they will stay with a brand for life.

Reward Brand Loyalty

KEEP GOOD RECORDS

The best loyalty programs involve ways to keep careful, complete records of every member's purchases, whether they make them in person, by phone, or online. Happily, you don't have to invent the technology to make this happen—it already exists, even if your business is small or local. Take a look at 360Incentives.com, Preferred Market Solutions, The Loyalty Box, LoyaltyGator, Zooz Solutions, CashFootprint, River Cities, or Appdator to find a package that fits your business.

GIVE THE CUSTOMER CHOICES

Every customer is different, so he should be able to choose his own reward. Back to Panera, their free-pastry bonus allows consumers to choose any pastry they like—they are not restricted to the peanut butter cookies, for example. Compare this to the Victoria's Secret loyalty program, which often restricts the reward to giving out a specific type of low-rise panties—something that only interests young, thin women. This kind of "prize" tells the rest of Victoria's Secret's clientele that the company does not value their patronage. (Overheard from a clerk at Victoria's Secret when a middle-aged woman noted that the panties gift was of no use to her: "Well, that's not really our fault, is it?")

WHAT CAN YOU OFFER?

Just about every major retailer, hotel chain, and restaurant has a loyalty program with a membership card these days. Why is everybody doing it? The simple answer is that it works. Loyalty programs give customers gifts, coupons, or automatic dollars off for making frequent or multiple purchases. Offering points for purchases, discounts at different point levels, and quick rewards for frequent visits are all effective ways to keep your customer base engaged, and to let them know you value their continuing business.

Think about the kinds of things you can offer customers for their continued patronage. If you run a bakery, a free muffin after 10 purchases can be enough to brighten someone's morning. If you're in the car repair business, your client could receive her tenth oil change free. Perhaps it's more appropriate for her to accumulate points for dollars spent, earning a coupon for $5 off her next purchase once she has spent over $100 with you. Whatever you choose, make the reward automatic, so she doesn't need to remember to bring a paper coupon to your business.

DON'T BE STINGY

You don't need to give away the store, but you do need to give your customers something they value to make them want to participate in your loyalty program. Panera Bread, for example, tracks customer purchases and provides small, incremental rewards after customers spend certain amounts over time. The rewards pop up at the register when the cashier swipes the loyalty card, so customers don't even have to remember that they've got a reward due on their next visit.

NO EXPIRATION DATE

Few things are more infuriating to customers than discovering that the points or stars they've accumulated will expire if they don't use them right away. Think of these points as if they were change in a jar: The change still has the same value, even if it sits there for a year or longer. Companies use expiration dates to create some urgency for customers to frequent their establishments, but this can backfire. When a client who believes she has accumulated 100,000 points tries to make a hotel reservation and discovers those points have expired (often without warning from the company), her vacation is ruined. Now you've made her angry, and she may never use your hotel chain again.

IF REWARDS MUST EXPIRE, WARN THE CUSTOMER

Some companies simply can't afford to let customers accumulate hundreds of thousands of points (even though this means they have spent a small fortune with them). If you need to set expiration dates, set up your system to send e-mail warnings six months in advance, to let patrons find a way to use the points before they disappear.

BIRTHDAYS AND SPECIAL OCCASIONS

Once a customer becomes a member of your program, you have the information you need to help him celebrate special events. Offer him a free gift with a short-term deadline on his birthday or anniversary, so he has only a week or two to decide how to use it.

SERVICES AS REWARDS

Rewards can come in many forms beyond gift cards and coupons. Neiman Marcus's InCircle program offers customers free shipping, entries into sweepstakes for big prizes, free alterations, dining at in-store restaurants, and occasional special gifts. At Best Buy, clients who reach the Premier Silver Level of their Reward Zone program get time with a Geek Squad consultant who helps them learn a new technology or effect a quick repair.

MORE THAN COFFEE

Offering something beyond the usual cup of coffee is the stock-in-trade of the Starbucks empire, and the company's loyalty program is one of the most effective you'll find anywhere. Not only do enrolled customers receive a free drink of their choice after 12 purchases (quantified as "stars"), but they also get surprises once a week or more: free song downloads, smartphone apps they might not come across on their own, and bonus stars for purchasing food items or bags of ground coffee. All of these come to them automatically through the Starbucks app, which they can also use to pay for their drinks.

CREATE A HIERARCHY

The Best Western Rewards program is one of the best in the affordable hotel industry, enabling clients to earn their way up a ladder of benefits based on the frequency with which they stay at Best Western hotels. At the program's higher levels, guests earn more points per stay, priority bookings, in-room gifts, and members-only special offers; at the very highest level, they even get a special number on which to reach a booking agent more quickly.

KEEP THE PROGRAM SIMPLE

Have you ever joined a loyalty program with so many rules that you couldn't keep track of all the ways to earn rewards? Programs that only reward certain kinds of purchases—for example, a hotel program that only awards points if the guest stays two nights or more, or if he has breakfast in the hotel restaurant—quickly become more trouble that they are worth for the client. You want to reward his frequent buying, not discourage him from earning his bonus or gift.

REWARD FOR EVERY PURCHASE

Some rewards programs are only good for full-price merchandise, meaning one has to forego sale or clearance items in order to accumulate points. This kind of restriction infuriates customers, who perceive the points as an incentive that doesn't actually cost the company any money. For the greatest impact and the most repeat business, give points for every purchase, no matter how much is spent or how deeply discounted the merchandise is. This works for Bloomingdale's, where points are awarded to customers who buy online, in their retail stores, and in their discount outlets.

INSIDER INTEL

Make your loyalty program members the first to know when you bring out your holiday items or introduce a new line of products. Giving them advance notice, creating launch dates and first-day celebrations, and providing samples of new products can excite these members, getting them talking to their friends and colleagues about what's new at your business.

DOUBLE THE POINTS

Special offers can drive business on specific days or for individual items. If you run an ice cream shop, for example, and you're introducing a new flavor, give double points to customers who order that flavor in any form (cone, dish, part of a sundae). If you're planning a holiday event, offer double points to all those who buy from you that day. The extra points will encourage them to buy more so they can accumulate lots of points and subsequent rewards.

PLENTY OF ACCESS

To make the most of their loyalty cards, customers need to know how many points they have and how close they are to their next reward. Give them access to the rewards system through your website, as well as through a smartphone or tablet app. The easier it is for them to determine how many points they have or when their next reward is coming, the more likely they are to return to your store to spend some more.

MEMBERS-ONLY OFFERS

Sephora is one retailer that really understands how a loyalty program works. Members of its Beauty Insider program can use their points to buy products available only to them, such as sample products, sets of products packaged specifically for the program, and free beauty classes or makeovers. Your company may have items or services such as these, that is, items or services that make loyal customers feel special or "elite," and also show them how much you value their continued business.

THINK BEYOND MERCHANDISE

One of the most interesting loyalty programs comes from Walgreens, where customers earn Balance Rewards by doing things to take care of themselves (including, of course, shopping at Walgreens). Program members earn points for prescriptions they fill or vaccinations they get at the pharmacy, and even for tracking their weight loss or getting more exercise. The points can be exchanged for gift cards to use in the store—and the better care you take of yourself, the larger those gift cards are. Walgreens gets customers to come back to them regularly, and they also get the brand identity boost that results from caring about their customers' health as well as their buying power.

REWARDS FOR TOTAL PURCHASES

If the Starbucks program is too large for your company to swallow, there are plenty of simpler ways to build loyalty through frequent purchases. Great Harvest Bread Company in upstate New York, for example, gives each enrolled customer a simple cardboard card that gets stamped every time she buys a loaf of fresh-baked bread. When her card reaches a dozen stamps, she gets the next loaf for free. It's simple, requires no bookkeeping on the bakery's part, and costs the company almost nothing to maintain.

ONLINE-ONLY PROGRAMS

If all of your business takes place online, your loyalty program
can be even easier to run. Customers sign up for rewards on
your website and at their leisure, so they can skip the often
tedious process of registering their loyalty card in a store
while others wait in line. Once registered, they can earn points
for doing just about anything on the site: filling out surveys,
responding to tweets, liking the company's Facebook page—
and, of course, buying merchandise.

AUTOMATIC REWARDS

Red Roof Inn's loyalty program sends out a paper certificate
every time a guest reaches five thousand points (roughly six
stays) on his RediCard. This simple, basic program keeps
customers from accumulating tens of thousands of points that
linger unused, and reminds them that they've got a free night
in hand—which may encourage them to book a longer stay. Best
Buy uses the same principle with its Reward Zone, a program
that awards customers a $5 gift card when they hit 250 points.

ACCESS TO PURCHASE INFORMATION

Have you ever found yourself trying to remember what hotel
you stayed at two years ago, or what style those pants were
that you bought last spring? Loyalty programs can enable your
customers to look up exactly where they stayed, what they
bought, and what style and size they chose, so they can make
repeat purchases of the exact same items. They will enjoy the
convenience and you'll have valuable information available if
you want to offer them catered sales. Everyone wins.

Building Loyalty Through Great Service

FOLLOWING UP

Let's say you've gone to an oral surgeon to have a wisdom tooth pulled out. Two days later, you notice you're experiencing a little more pain than you expected, but you brush the concern aside and continue stoically through your day. It would not occur to you to call the doctor—you don't want to sound like you "can't take it." Remarkably, your phone rings. It's the surgeon's office, checking in to see how you feel and if you need any pain medication. How did they know? They do this every day, so of course they know . . . and they also know some patients won't admit that they're in pain. That's the kind of customer service that makes people remember you.

Your business may not have suffering patients, but you can take a lesson from this basic service of most surgical practices. If you know a customer made a purchase that might require a little extra advice, give her a call. She will hardly believe her ears, and will tell her friends about your great follow-up.

A THANK-YOU CARD

Follow-up can demonstrate, in a simple way, that you appreciate a customer's business—something most companies forget about. Sending a quick, handwritten note is a top-of-the-line gesture of true gratitude. The fact that you took a moment to say thank you will impress just about any patron.

JUST SAY THANKS—DON'T ASK FOR ANYTHING IN RETURN

Don't send a thank-you card as another way to get business from a client. Including a coupon that requires an additional purchase, a survey card, a stack of your business cards, or anything else for him to hand out or use on your behalf negates the value of the note. You can always send coupons or a comment card a week later or by e-mail, but let your thanks stand on their own.

GIVE YOUR REGULARS A LITTLE EXTRA

You run a hair salon, and a regular client looks like she's having a rough week. Her skin seems sallow, and you can feel the tension in her neck. Send over your nail technician to give her a hand massage, free of charge, and offer her a treatment with a new hair product that will make her tresses shine. Make up a package of samples that she can take home with her. You've brightened her day and made her feel better about herself, and it didn't cost you anything but time.

BE THERE FOR THE CUSTOMER

The research company Genesys has found that customers overwhelmingly prefer speaking to a living, breathing human being about their problems than using any other method of communication. (Incidentally, voice self-service got the lowest marks of any service option.) Just making live customer service reps available can put your company far out ahead of your competition. The more—and more frequent—access customers get to live service, the better they will feel about your company's ability to address their issues.

DEMONSTRATE HOW IT WORKS

You can show customers you're committed to their satisfaction with your products by taking the time to show them how they work. Upfront, in-person training will help them get on board with a given item faster, and therefore get more out of it sooner. If you're selling widescreen televisions in a store, for instance, stand with customers and show them how to use all the great new features on the remote before they leave with their new purchase. If you're dealing with a tablet computer, power it up and talk them through using it for the first time.

INTRODUCE CUSTOMERS TO NEW IDEAS

We said we'd mention Wegmans again—the eastern United States supermarket chain that has revolutionized the usability of a grocery store. In the produce area at every one of their stores, a chef in a toque and a white coat demonstrates recipes involving potentially unfamiliar vegetables, and encourages shoppers to "Strive for 5"—five servings of fruits and vegetables per day. Customers can taste what the chef makes, and pick up the corresponding recipe and ingredients right there at his station. Not only do they learn new cooking techniques, but they also discover foods they didn't even know they liked. Remarkably, Brussels sprouts became one of Wegman's big sellers in the produce department after company chefs showed customers how to make them taste great.

Similarly, you can turn your patrons on to new concepts by demonstrating them in-store, and then providing all the tools and information they need to put them into practice at home. You will sell more products, and your customers will see you as a go-to expert when it comes to such things.

RECOGNIZE PROBLEMS AND CORRECT THEM

You've introduced the next version of your software. About three days after your customers download it, your service department starts getting calls—and they're all about the same issue. After the fourth call, your service manager comes over and explains the situation. What's your next move?

If you have a small customer base, you can send them an e-mail right away, letting them know that you're aware of the problem and you're working on it. If you've got thousands of customers, though, you need to use some other means to reach them. Let it be known on your website, Twitter, and other social media that you're coming up with a solution (see the story about Buffer in Part Five, page 165). Your customers just want you to be proactive—they know software bugs are a fact of life, and what distinguishes good companies from bad ones is the way in which they handle their discovery, research, and repair.

ASK FOR FEEDBACK, AND LISTEN WHEN YOU GET IT

A responsive company solicits feedback from customers and takes it to heart. The more you know about what your customers think of your company and your products, the better you can respond with new products, updates, and innovations that satisfy their needs.

Social media (more on this in Part Seven) has largely replaced the Comments boxes stores once had, so make sure you're on all the platforms customers now use to tell you what they think—and, of course, be sure to look at what they're posting. Ask your salespeople what they know or hear, as well. You may get some great clues to what the next big thing in your industry should be.

COMPETENCE BREEDS SATISFACTION

The Genesys study mentioned earlier discovered another useful fact: Subjects said their most satisfying customer service experiences had come from interactions with competent representatives.

Friendliness and a gift for conversation will help an interaction get off to a great start, but in the end, every person dealing with your customers needs a strong working knowledge of your products and services. Training your staff is a key investment in keeping clients, whether you have minimum-wage employees at a fast-food counter, or technology experts in a business-to-business organization.

NOT JUST HAPPY, BUT IN LOVE

Wouldn't it be great if your customers told their friends, family members, and coworkers how much they loved your company? Lots of businesses make customers happy, but love is much harder to attain. A company that manages to inspire love does it by engaging its customers on an emotional level that goes well beyond great products; it shows them that it understands them and has a vested interest in their lives.

Trader Joe's, for example, does this by publicizing its folksy hipster culture with a newsprint magazine, old-fashioned label designs, workers in Hawaiian shirts, and products that blend ingredients and flavors in ways that seem reductively natural. These products often come with relatable stories about the people who made them, whisking away any hint of pretension—and somehow making a multinational grocery chain seem downhome. It's important to note that Trader Joe's has neither a loyalty program nor sales and discounts, yet its customers are so fiercely loyal that if they can't shop there, they just won't shop.

CREATING A MEMORABLE EXPERIENCE

In a study conducted by global research firm Gfk, 61 percent of subjects said they were less loyal to any one retailer, because they shopped around to find the best value. Why is this happening, despite all the loyalty programs and rewards meant to entice customers to return? Gfk suggests that most do not have memorable experiences with the companies from which they buy products and services. Good experiences elicit strong, positive emotions that make customers remember what you did and how it made them feel. If their experience is so neutral that it creates no lasting memory, they will feel no compelling reason to come back. Indeed, if all experiences are interchangeable, all that's left is shopping on price.

WHAT MAKES A POSITIVE MEMORY?

Many kinds of shopping and buying experiences make good memories for consumers:

- Trying free samples
- Receiving a special gift with a purchase
- Having a pleasant chat with a salesperson
- Looking and feeling attractive during a dressing room experience
- Having the opportunity to linger and browse without pressure
- Getting a great solution to a nagging problem
- Getting help from a knowledgeable salesperson who did not make them feel foolish

THE MOST IMPORTANT WAY TO BE MEMORABLE

The Gfk study suggests that consumers would be more loyal to a brand or retailer if they had the opportunity to give input, or to help shape the products or services they buy.

How can you involve your customers more and give them the chance to influence the kinds of products you create or carry? Ask them. Every time a customer completes a transaction, ask what they would like to see or what they wish they could buy there. You may be amazed at the scope and breadth of responses you get, and the insights you gather will help you plan what comes next for your company.

COMMENT CARDS AND SURVEYS

Nothing beats personal interaction, but if you want to get a solid record of your customers' opinions and ideas for your next round of products and services, surveys can be cost-effective and easy to use.

Place a comment card or simple survey in the bag with your customer's purchase, or put one at every table in your restaurant with a pencil people can use to fill it out. If your clients buy from you online, a pop-up survey at the end of the transaction can gather this information for you.

If you keep a database of their e-mail addresses, send them a link to a survey online or ask them directly what they'd like to see from your company. Inexpensive tools like SurveyMonkey enable you to poll your customers quickly and easily and receive the compiled information in real time at any point during the survey period.

GIFT WRAPPING

Remember when department stores would wrap gifts for you free of charge? It's been too long since this custom was abandoned. Some stores can make a standard purchase in a bag look like a lovely gift in minutes; all they have to do is add some tissue paper and ribbon. Bring in extra workers during holiday shopping times—at Mother's and Father's Day and Valentine's, as well as during Christmas season—to perform this kind and simple gesture for your customers. If they prefer to buy gift cards, put these in special envelopes or small boxes, to make them look like exciting gifts.

ANOTHER WAY TO BE MEMORABLE

When we talk about customer service, we can't help but talk about Southwest Airlines, a company that seems to have a strong understanding of what customers want. A comfortable flight and an on-time departure and arrival are basics for the airline, and when it can't deliver because of weather, airport issues, or the occasional equipment problem, it gives customers an LUV voucher that they can apply toward their next reservation. It's not a free ticket, but it doesn't have to be; the simple gesture acknowledges the inconvenience, whether or not it could have been avoided by the airline. The moral of the story: If you can't deliver a perfect experience to your customer, let him know that you know, and make a reasonable effort to make things right.

GENUINE CARING

Let's say a young mother comes into your bookstore and wants to find the perfect book for her three-year-old's birthday. You have two choices: You can wave her over to the children's book area and let her browse on her own, or you can ask some questions about the child and his interests. Does he like animals? Is he learning to count? Does he already have all the Dr. Seuss books he can use? Does he prefer trucks, dinosaurs, monsters, or stories about little boys like him? You can battle the online bookstores by taking a genuine interest in your customer and the recipient of the gift, making the experience of buying at your store as helpful, pleasant, and memorable as you possibly can.

YOUR EFFORT INSTEAD OF THE CUSTOMER'S TIME

In this world of mobile communications, you can grant your customers the luxury of time while fulfilling their request. A Macy's customer told DailyFinance.com that she went to Macy's looking for an item she knew they carried, but it was not on the shelf. The salesperson said she would search the stock room and call the customer on her mobile phone when she found it. Sure enough, several hours later the customer got the phone call. In the interim, she was free to enjoy her shopping day instead of standing around waiting.

BASIC COURTESY

In our modern world, it's easy to forget how nice it is to have someone open a door for you or help you carry your packages—which is why such basic demonstrations of courtesy can make a customer's experience with your company so memorable. Keep an eye out for opportunities to treat customers as you would treat your mom, by swinging open a door, hanging up a coat, placing items in a dressing room to try on later, fetching a different size, or pulling out and pushing in a chair.

HELP CUSTOMERS HELP ONE ANOTHER

Tech-savvy customers often want to find a quick fix for a problem online, rather than wait on hold with a call center. Apple has forums that enable such customers to talk to one another, and some Apple "geniuses" monitor these forums to help solve odd but recurring problems. The fact that Apple is involved in this way helps it retain its reputation for service, and allows smart users to benefit from the knowledge others like them bring to the site.

PLEASURE, NOT PRESSURE

What separates the experience of buying a BMW from that of buying a Hyundai? The cheaper the car is, the more likely it is you will meet a high-pressure salesperson who wants to get you into it that day. No business should emulate that kind of customer experience in the twenty-first century. Instead, look to the BMW dealership with its luxurious showroom, relaxed salespeople, and plenty of time to get to know the customer—all in all, a memorable experience for all the right reasons.

GIVE THEM SOMETHING (GOOD) TO TALK ABOUT

The Toronto research firm The Verde Group determined that four out of five shoppers will tell an average of three other people about a great customer experience. In addition, for 63 percent of shoppers, a great experience comes from the level of engagement of the employees who help them—in particular, from their politeness and good manners. We can expand this to just about anyone in customer service: call center employees, cable guys, advertising account executives, public servants, and many more. Nothing sells like a person who is pleasant and interested in what the customer has to say.

MAKE GETTING OUT AS EASY AS GETTING IN

When a customer called Life Alert to let the company know her mother was going into a nursing home and would no longer need the service, she was surprised to discover that the voice prompt system actually offered this as one of the choices. Pressing the right number to reach the cancellation desk, she spoke with a helpful, sympathetic employee who expedited the service disconnection. This employee did not try to talk her out of the cancellation or sell her additional services, therby making a difficult time as easy and smooth as possible for her. "They even told me I didn't have to return the equipment—they asked me to recycle it responsibly," she said. "I would recommend this company to anyone."

SIT AND LISTEN

Many businesses don't have the customer contact opportunities found in retail or hospitality, so they have to make an occasion to connect with their clients. If you work in business-to-business service, ask your customer if you can bring your lunch over one day and just spend some time listening to what people at his firm or company have to say about their industry. Take notes and ask questions; find out what this company needs in general, while also thinking about what you might be able to provide more specifically. This is not the day to make a presentation or a sales pitch—it's an opportunity for you to listen to your customers, and learn how to better tailor your services to their needs.

NOW, TAKE IT ALL TO HEART

You can listen to your customers for hours on end, but real proof that you've heard them will come from your changing, updating, or modifying your offerings based on what they've told you. If they've told you that they want to see chicken breasts packaged individually in freezable packages, start packaging your chicken breasts that way—and tell them you are doing so. If they want you to get rid of Styrofoam and pack everything in recyclable containers, do it and announce it to them. When they know you've heard their concerns and changed the way you do business to suit them, your new bond with them will be hard to break.

Going Beyond the Extra Mile

NORDSTROM OF THE LEGEND

When a shopper's brother's home burned to the ground, she went to Nordstrom to pick up housewares and other items to help him and his family get back on their feet. She hooked up with a salesperson who walked her through various departments until they had gathered the essentials. At that point, the salesperson asked her to wait a moment and went into the back room. When she came out, she announced to the customer that her $500-plus tab was on the store. The management also offered to wrap everything up for free shipping.

THE STARBUCKS EXPERIENCE

It's not uncommon for Starbucks to hand out store credit for less-than-perfect experiences reported to its corporate offices, but one customer in particular claims the company made him very happy: When he called to complain about a bad interaction with a barista, Starbucks not only refunded the cost of his drink, but also fueled his rewards card with a $50 bonus. The explanation: Starbucks wanted his experience to be "nothing short of fantastic."

THE LEGO LESSON

Not long after spending all of his Christmas money on a Lego Ultrasonic Raider set, seven-year-old Luka lost the Jay ZX minifigure when it fell out of his pocket at the grocery store. He e-mailed Lego to ask if they could send him a new one, promising never to take the figure out of the house again. The e-mail he received from Richard in Lego Customer Service explained that Richard had consulted Sensei Wu, a master in the Ninjago universe, and that Sensei had given him permission to send Luka a new Jay—along with a bad guy for him to fight. The Sensei also reminded Luka to keep his minifigures safe.

THE WESTJET CHRISTMAS MIRACLE

In December 2013, in an astonishing act of ingenuity, coordination, and holiday magic, the Canadian firm WestJet Airlines chose two flights' worth of passengers to receive the Christmas gifts they had been offered to request from Santa just before they boarded their planes for Calgary, Alberta. The airline planted a virtual Santa in each airport, directing the passengers to chat with him on camera and tell him what they wanted for Christmas. When they landed in Calgary, they were taken to a special baggage claim area, where their requested gifts arrived on the carousel before their luggage did—everything from socks and underwear to widescreen televisions. WestJet made a video of the entire event, and promised to donate flights to families in need through Ronald MacDonald House Charities if 200,000 people viewed the video. As of the time of this writing, the video on YouTube has received more than 40 million views. (You can see it at https://www.youtube.com/watch?v=zIEIvi2MuEk.)

SOUTHWEST LOCATES A MISSING BAG

It may have happened to you: A bag did not arrive with your flight. For Lisa Chapman, that meant being stuck in "a tiny town two hours outside of Kansas City," where she had flown for a family reunion, with no change of clothing or makeup. Luckily, she had flown Southwest Airlines, a company whose name has become synonymous with great customer service. A baggage office employee named Mina tracked down her bag, which had been picked up by accident by another passenger at baggage claim and driven to Branson, Missouri. She kept Lisa updated on the bag's progress back to Kansas City, and had it delivered to her two hours after it arrived there. She had promised Lisa she'd have it by 11 a.m., and she delivered. "Even though it's been inconvenient (hey, nothing's perfect), thanks to Mina, I feel great about Southwest Airlines," Lisa wrote on her Marketing and Social Media blog.

THE RESTROOM SAVE

Leave it to Twitter to connect a train passenger with toilet paper at a critical moment. When a young man named Adam found himself trapped in a train car restroom without a way to wipe, he tweeted the train company, Virgin Trains, and let them know exactly which train he was riding. Two minutes later, Virgin tweeted back to ask which coach he was in, and in a moment Adam received the much-needed roll. This may just be the best use of social media technology *ever*.

A GIFT FROM THE GAYLORD

A guest at the Gaylord Opryland Hotel in Nashville, Tennessee, admired the clock radio in her room—a white noise machine that also played music so relaxing she decided she wanted to buy one to take home. The device was exclusive to the hotel, but staff directed her to a similar one at Sharper Image. This one didn't play the same music, however, and she tweeted this to the hotel while thanking the management for their help. To her surprise, she received a package in her room later that day: it was the desired clock radio with the spa music—and the hotel's compliments, of course.

KINDLE MAYDAY BUTTON TOPS TABLET FEATURES

Personalized, face-to-face service from a human being on a digital device? When Amazon introduced its Mayday button on its Kindle Fire HDX tablet, it beat all the other tablet manufacturers to the punch. Going way beyond the iPhone's Siri and Microsoft's Cortana voice recognition features, Kindle Fire's Mayday puts users in touch with a live person, 24 hours a day, 365 days a year, at the touch of a button. What's more, this person communicates through real-time video chat, actually allowing users to see whom they're talking with. So far, your Mayday friend can't see you, but she can still help you through whatever procedure you need on your tablet, and she'll stick with you until all of your questions are answered.

LEXUS HANDS OUT NEW CARS

A product recall in 2006 apparently embarrassed Lexus, one of the top luxury car brands, more than the company could stand. When car owners came into the dealerships to get their recalled parts replaced, the company didn't remove the parts or fix their cars—instead, it gave each of them a brand new Lexus free of charge. Chances are most of them will be driving Lexus vehicles for the rest of their lives.

ANYTHING FOR A NORDSTROM CUSTOMER

When a security staff member spotted a woman crawling around on the floor in a Nordstrom store, he went over immediately to see if he could help her. She said a diamond had fallen out of her wedding ring, and she was desperate to find it. He enlisted a team of people to search for it, and eventually the diamond was found: A staff member sifting through the dirt in the vacuum cleaner's bag located the missing gem.

SAINSBURYME TIME, ZAP

Three-year-old Lily observed one day that the "tiger" bread her parents had bought in Sainsbury's, a grocery store in the UK, looked more like the spotted coat of a giraffe. She wrote this in a letter to the store's management, and they decided they agreed with her. The bread was renamed "giraffe bread," and Lily got a letter back with a gift card. "I think renaming tiger bread giraffe bread is a brilliant idea," wrote customer service manager Chris King.

ZAPPOS DOES IT AGAIN

Social media is clogged with stories of the extraordinary customer service at Zappos, the online shoe and clothing store. Here's one that widens readers' eyes: When a customer's mother had medical treatments that left her feet numb and her shoes mostly useless, the daughter ordered six new pairs of shoes for her on Zappos. The mother chose the one pair that worked for her, and then called to find out how to return the other five. In the course of the call, she explained why she had to return such a large order. Two days later, a large bouquet of flowers arrived from Zappos, along with a card wishing her a speedy recovery.

WATCH FOR THE JETBLUE PEOPLE OFFICER

JetBlue employs a so-called People Officer: someone with the power to distribute free tickets to anyone he pleases. Providing entertainment during selected flights (never announced ahead of time, of course), the People Officer will conduct trivia games and offer winners free tickets to anywhere the airline flies. After the games, he'll ask passengers if they have questions or concerns about JetBlue, and he'll answer them all in detail. A pleasant surprise and some entertainment value can go a long way with customers.

IN A PINCH, TRADER JOE'S DELIVERS

When an 89-year-old man got snowed in at his Pennsylvania home right around Christmas time, his daughter called every grocery store in the area to find someone who would deliver food to his door. Trader Joe's stepped up to the plate—and after the woman placed the order, the manager told her that the whole thing, including delivery, would be free of charge. He wished her a Merry Christmas and had the groceries at her father's door just thirty minutes later. We can safely guess that this family will shop at Trader Joe's for many years to come.

UNITED AIRLINES COMES THROUGH FOR AN AUTHOR

When bestselling author Steven Levitt was on his way to catch a flight on United Airlines, he received a surprise call from customer service. They told him they could see he was in the airport (presumably, he had checked in at the ticket counter), and that the flight he was supposed to take was delayed. If he was willing to hurry a bit, though, they could get him on an earlier flight that would leave in forty minutes. This is the second such incident Levitt has enjoyed with United, and he credits both to his loyalty to the airline and its customer-centric policies.

THE LEGEND OF RITZ-CARLTON

Ritz-Carlton has long been considered the world's top organization when it comes to customer service. There are all kinds of stories about its employees going above and beyond for their guests. This one appeared in *Business Week*: A couple arriving at the hotel in Bali carried special eggs and milk for their son, who had complex food allergies. When they arrived, they discovered their supplies were spoiled. The hotel manager could not find the products locally, but the executive chef knew they were available in Singapore. He called his mother-in-law, who bought the products and then flew to Bali to deliver them—thus saving the day for both the child and his family.

REASON TO FLY OUT OF BALTIMORE

If you leave your car in the Airport Fast Park at the Baltimore-Washington Airport, you may find the experience to be a lot more pleasant than you expected. A parking lot attendant will guide you to the closest parking space, and then the shuttle will come to your car so you don't need to drag your luggage to a shelter yards away. The driver will help with your luggage, hold an umbrella for you if it's raining, and chat with you about your travel plans until he drops you at your departure terminal. Compare that to other airports, and you may wonder why the whole parking industry hasn't picked up on this kind of service.

CONNECTING TO POISON CONTROL

This story is partially horrifying, but it ends well. A dog owner panicked when she discovered that her pet had eaten ten Claritin pills. When she called the poison control hotline, the attendant told her it would cost her $65 to talk to a veterinarian. Luckily, however, Claritin is manufactured by Schering-Plough, and the company pays for any calls in which its products are involved. The dog owner contacted them and got connected to poison control right away, for free. (Woe to those whose dogs swallow a generic product.)

MORTON'S DELIVERS

When social media business consultant Peter Shankman got on a plane to go home to New York City, he expected to be starving by the time he got there. As a joke, he tweeted, "Hey, @Mortons, can you meet me at newark airport with a porterhouse when I land in two hours? K, thanks. ;)." Luckily for Peter, Morton's got the tweet and met him at Newark: A man in a tuxedo handed him a shopping bag with his Porterhouse steak and some potatoes, bread, a shrimp cocktail, and even napkins and silverware.

A BREAKOUT MOVE BY CVS

Although it has a commitment to health so strong that it stopped selling tobacco products in 2014, CVS is not normally connected with highway safety. But it turns out the company has had "Samaritan vans" on the road for more than thirty years, watching for stranded motorists and bringing them the help they need. The vans don't charge for their services. Recipients of their help are asked only to fill out a comment card and send it to the pharmacy chain's management.

TACO BELL MAKES GOOD IN ALASKA

In June 2012, someone played a cruel joke on the bush town of Bethel, Alaska, posting fliers that claimed Taco Bell would soon open a fast food restaurant in the six-thousand-person town. It took only a couple of weeks for radio station KYUK to determine that these rumors were a hoax, but in the meantime, it alerted the company's stores in Anchorage—and Anchorage carried the news back to corporate headquarters. Learning of the crushing disappointment in Bethel, Taco Bell took it upon itself to airlift a food truck filled with ingredients for ten thousand tacos to the tiny town. How much food is that? The truck contained 950 pounds of beef, 500 pounds of sour cream, and a combined 600 pounds of lettuce and tomatoes, just for starters.

PART

CUSTOMER SERVICE
ONLINE

Are you connecting with your customers on Twitter and Facebook? Does your website provide opportunities for direct feedback on your products and services? Are you running forums so that customers can talk to one another and get immediate help on their technical questions?

If the answer to any of the above is "no," then you may not be using social media to your best advantage. In the age of digital communication, instant messaging, and open contact between companies and customers, you need to establish an online presence beyond your website in order to take advantage of some of the most rewarding ways to build relationships with clients.

That being said, social media can be a minefield of missteps that could potentially blow up in your face. Customers can take a misguided retort from your company and plaster it all over the Internet, making it nearly impossible for you to remove and recover from. They can bring their smartphones into your store, restaurant, or other establishment and record your employees as they misbehave—or one of your customers as she makes a scene. They know that if they simply threaten to make an incriminating video and "have it go viral," you have no real way of knowing whether the threat is credible or not..

It's a brave new world, and it's time for you to learn how to find your way around it. This part provides tips to help you understand the commitment you need to make to social media, how to make them work for you, and what to do when they work against you.

Twitter, Facebook, Instagram, and the Social Media Revolution

LEARN HOW TO USE TWITTER

If you don't have a Twitter account, creating one is easier than you may think. Go to www.twitter.com and sign up using the name of your business as your handle (that's your username). Pick something that will make yourself very easy to find (so, Joe's Meats becomes @JoesMeats, and Finger Lakes Tourism becomes @TourFingerLakes). Add a profile photo; this will show up next to your handle every time you tweet, so choose something striking and appropriate. Write a bio for your business in 160 characters or less. Add a link to your website, then upload a header image—a photo that will appear at the top of your own Twitter page, showcasing your business or one of your capabilities. That's it! Now you're ready to start connecting with customers.

There are plenty of tutorials online to teach you how to use Twitter (including the one at support.twitter.com, and our personal favorite, momthisishowtwitterworks.com). Once you know how to manage your account, start attracting followers by letting your customers know you're there: Post signs in your store locations, put table tents on your restaurant tables, list your Twitter handle in your e-mail newsletter, and put it on all of your employees' business cards.

UNDERSTANDING CUSTOMERS AND SOCIAL MEDIA

A study by social media marketing firm Sprout Social revealed some useful facts about customer service and online requests for information: Consumer social media messages demanding company response increased by 77 percent in 2014. The largest growth took place in the government sector, but Internet and technology companies as well as professional services have seen a dramatic growth in the number of consumer messages they receive through social media.

Here's the most important part: Five out of six of these messages go unanswered. Think how easy it could be for your company to shine in this scenario. All you have to do is answer your customers' questions.

MAKE A FAST START WITH TWITTER

When it comes to reaching out to companies for quick answers, Twitter may be on the verge of replacing the telephone. Customers choose to communicate this way because it eliminates the need to wade through voice prompts or sit in a hold queue. They simply ask a straight question and get a straight answer—no fuss, no tedious queries about their e-mail address and phone number. Your mission, should you accept it, is to have staff members monitor Twitter day and night and respond to all questions with useful answers. If you can do this, you will delight your customers.

FOLLOW OTHERS ON TWITTER

To begin the conversation, you need to build up a list of followers and tweet to them regularly—and not just in order to sell them products. You also need to be on the lookout for tweets and other messages from them, so you can respond to these on the spot.

The best way to start racking up Twitter followers is to start following people you find interesting. Most of them will follow you back, so you'll build your followers and get exposed to more people. To build followers beyond your current customers, start looking for people who have interests that may be compatible with your business. Twitter offers more than 350 interest categories to help you find people who match the customer profile you built according to the instructions in Part Two. You can also target people who follow your followers based on their handles, the interests they describe in their profiles, and key words that appear in their tweets.

START TWEETING

People will only see you when you tweet, so start talking about your business and your offerings. Write messages of no more than 140 characters (spaces count) with news people can use. Do you have new seasonal offerings? Did you just land a new client? Did something fun happen in the store today? Have you got a new flavor, side dish, delivery truck, booking for your band? Tell your followers interesting things that only an expert like you would know, and post links to favorite pages or articles that you think will be of interest to potential customers. Whatever you have to talk about, tweet it and see what happens. Keep your tweets to a maximum of one or two a day, unless something important is going on that you need to "live tweet" about as it happens.

WHAT CAN HAPPEN?

You may get messages from customers or potential customers, asking you questions about things you offer. You might receive tweets from fans of your products or services. You could get special requests, like the one Adam sent to @VirginTrains (see Part Six) that resulted in his receiving a roll of toilet paper at a crucial moment. In some cases, you might get "flamed" (that is, receive complaints, insults, and other trash talk) for something you, your company, or one of your employees did—or something someone out there believes you did.

It's also possible that nothing at all will happen, especially if no one follows you. Like any other marketing and customer service activity, what you get out of it will depend on how much you're willing to put into it.

GET READY FOR THE 24/7/365 UNIVERSE

Social media never sleeps. If you don't believe it, check out Facebook and Twitter some night in the wee hours, when you're binge-watching six episodes of your favorite TV show and you've lost track of time. You're not the only one awake, and even if your business is strictly local, you may get inquiries when you think everyone should be asleep. This doesn't mean someone tweeting you at 3 a.m. local time really expects you to be available to answer questions, but it's something to keep in mind when you start work in the morning. Check Facebook, Twitter, and any other platform you're using, and respond to any queries that may have come in overnight, especially during your peak seasons.

TRENDING AND HASHTAGS

When lots of people are talking about your business at once, it becomes a hot topic of conversation—in Twitter-speak, that's called trending. Twitter posts a short list of trending topics that can change from second to second, depending on how many people are discussing the same thing at the same time. To figure out what's trending, the Twitter algorithm tracks key words (like March Madness or Oscar nominations) as well as hashtags—phrases that begin with a #—that help people talking about the same thing find one another. You can find out which hashtags are trending and join those conversations simply by searching for a specific phrase (for example, #chocoholic, #winelovers, or #BarackObama) and seeing what comes up. If you know that a specific hashtag is trending, you can just click on it on Twitter's short list and get a long list of tweets about it.

TWITTER IS TWO-WAY COMMUNICATION

Twitter is a useful tool because people who tweet can reach your company in seconds and get a quick response to any question, or tell you when they have a problem and get it resolved in minutes. They can do this because Twitter sends alerts to your smartphone (or, more likely, the smartphone of your social media director or director of communications), so there's no reason to ever miss a tweet directed at you.

If you're still using a phone that's just a phone, it's time to upgrade to one of the many smartphones on the market. Download the Twitter app, go to your Settings, and select the option that allows Twitter to send you these alerts. Now you're ready to communicate at any time, anywhere, with anyone who tweets you about anything.

COORDINATE THE MESSAGE

It's great to get tweets from customers wanting to know when you'll have the next new Lego set in stock or if your restaurant has gluten-free menu items, but not every tweet you get will be chatty, complimentary, or fun.

Just ask Qantas Airlines, which rolled out a Twitter campaign with the hashtag #QantasLuxury just a day after its entire fleet was grounded because of a labor dispute. Not only was this an enormous failure of communication between the airline's top management and whoever handled social media for them, but it also turned a fun campaign into a public relations nightmare. Qantas meant for the campaign to encourage people to tweet about how they had been pampered when flying on the airline, but instead their hashtag got hijacked and used against them. "Loyal and competent staff, paid accordingly, proud to work for you, not being screwed over by management #QantasLuxury," one tweet read. Another tweet: "Couriers to make sure my staff around the world get their lockout notices any hour of the day or night #QantasLuxury."

What can we learn from this? Make sure your social media efforts are coordinated throughout the company, so everyone knows when today is not the day to tweet.

USE SOCIAL MEDIA TO DIRECT TRAFFIC

If Twitter's 140-character limit seems too short to tell any kind of useful story, use your postings to direct readers to more information. Add a live link to the end of your post to bring people to the rest of the news or information you want them to receive. You can track the click-through traffic using your website metrics app, to see exactly how effective your original post was in encouraging people to learn more.

YOU CAN'T CONTROL HASHTAGS

Here's the truth about using Twitter: Anyone can take your hashtag and use it any way she likes. No matter how positive you meant to be with your clever message, someone else on Twitter can use your hashtag to mean exactly the opposite. One of the best examples of this is #McDStories, a hashtag meant to introduce good-news tales of farmers and other high-quality suppliers from whom McDonald's buys its ingredients. When the company started telling its own McDStories on Twitter, however, those who had a bone to pick with them took the hashtag and ran with it. @Alice_2112 tweeted, "Hospitalized for food poisoning after eating McDonald's in 1989. Never ate there again and became a vegetarian. Should have sued. #McDStories." Countless others chimed in with stories of equal severity. McDonald's was powerless to stop the onslaught.

MISTAKES CAN LINGER, EVEN IF YOU DELETE THEM

Let's talk for a moment about the curious case of Congressman Anthony Weiner's indelicate underpants photo. Weiner used Twitter to send a scantily clad photo of himself to a follower in Seattle, and then removed the photo once it became clear that his poor judgment had gone public. Removing the photo made no difference, however, because of the wonders of modern technology: Every news media outlet had a screenshot of it, as did just about anyone else who took an interest once the story began to break. While Weiner had sent the photo privately to one person, it became a national media phenomenon.

Don't post anything online that you would't want the entire world to see. Even if it's up there only for a few minutes, a juicy mistake can become headline news in almost no time at all.

TWITTER'S GOOD SIDE

Here's why you need to get alerts from Twitter right away, no matter when they come through: Some communications with your customers and potential customers will lead directly to sales. Even if the correspondence in question does not result in a sale, the fact that your company is responsive to questions and requests will impress your followers—and they will remember that your company takes care of its clients day and night.

WHY YOU NEED TO BE ON FACEBOOK

Your Facebook page may someday eliminate the need for a website. Easy to build and maintain, and simple for your customers to find, a Facebook page for your business can include photos, messages, information on your background, hours and location, and just about anything else you may want to put up there. Your Facebook postings reach your audience in real time, so if your restaurant just ran out of this evening's fish special, you can let customers know immediately—and if your pastry chef just completed a spectacular cake for a wedding later that day, you can snap a quick photo with your phone and have it up in no time.

Like all social media, the conversation goes both ways. People who "like" your company's page can post to it, sharing great experiences or asking questions. Others can post complaints, bad reviews, accusations, and other negative messages if they choose—but, as the owner of the page, you can delete these postings if you wish, and block those who wrote them from ever posting there again. If only the rest of the Internet worked like Facebook, companies could clean up their images in minutes instead of paying expensive public relations firms to do it for them.

INSTAGRAM: THE VISUAL MEDIUM

If you're looking to capture the attention of a young adult audience, Instagram can help you do this with a remarkably small amount of effort: You just take a photo, modify it if you wish, and then add a brief caption before posting it to your page. It all takes a few seconds. If your company makes a product that is visually interesting, or if it is somehow related to travel, the outdoors, cooking and food, or other topics that interest young adults aged 18 to 35, you can draw lots of attention through Instagram. It's really that simple.

INSTAGRAM ADVERTISING

While companies can certainly use Instagram the same way individual users do, sponsored (paid) campaigns on the site may be the best way for you to introduce a new product or draw attention to your business. For example, Ben & Jerry's introduced its Scotchy Scotch Scotch flavor on the site using targeted ads that ran three times daily, and consequently achieved a 17 percent increase in the number of people who were aware of their delicious new item. The ads reached more than 9 million people in the United States.

Unlike standard ads on some social media sites, Instagram ads allow people to comment on your photo and caption, giving you an immediate sense of their response—good or bad—to your product or service. If you choose to use the site, you'll need to monitor it closely so you can respond to comments and answer questions as people encounter your ads.

REPRESENT YOUR COMPANY
ON LINKEDIN

By using LinkedIn, you can showcase your experience and business acumen to potentially thousands of future customers. You have the opportunity to post articles and respond to questions from people who may not be your clients today, but who may need your services in the future. Join forums and groups in your field; show members how responsive you can be to queries and how much valuable information and assistance you and your company can provide them with.

Keep an eye on forums, as well as on the articles or blogs that your prospects write, so you know right away if your company becomes a topic of conversation or if you can jump into a discussion and help.

REACH THE FRINGES ON GOOGLE+

Do you need to be on Google+? Google introduced this social networking site in 2011, and it may be popular among some Android smartphone users . . . but generally, it has not taken off the way Facebook, Pinterest, and Twitter have. In fact, in 2014, the annual Social Media Traffic Report by Shareholic indicated that Google+ drives just 0.08% of social referrals, versus Facebook's 21.25%. That being said, you may reach an audience here that you will not find anywhere else—specifically, people who don't like all the ads and sponsored content on Facebook. What does this tell you about the users at Google+? On the whole, they don't like companies that invade their creative space. Tread lightly if you're going to post a company profile here and try to reach out to customers. Offer assistance when people ask for it, not flashy messaging, and be part of the conversation instead of pushing your marketing message.

CHECK FOURSQUARE

This location program enables users to tell friends where they are at any given moment through smartphone alerts. If your business exists in the brick-and-mortar world, it's already on FourSquare—and if it's a restaurant, boutique, coffee shop, health club, or other business that warrants reviewing, you may be getting comments on it. Visit FourSquare's website (www.foursquare.com) and sign up for access to your business's profile and "tips"—recommendations left by customers during or after their visit. Perhaps the tips will be overwhelmingly positive, but you should be prepared for negatives, notes that tell people what to avoid on your menu, or what they did not like about their visit. If you can change these things, do it—and then go back to FourSquare and tell customers on your Profile page that their input helped you make things better. You may get some of them to try your store again.

GO MULTIMEDIA WITH TUMBLR

Claiming to host more than 200 million blogs, Tumblr lets users—including businesses—create pages with photos, videos, text, artwork, and more, expressing their originality through collages of visuals and sounds. You can create a company page here and load it up with all kinds of fascinating visuals, from videos of your product in action to photos of customers using it and enjoying the experience. This is a great place to advertise your products, and to connect with customers who may ask you questions or look for information. The site is ridiculously easy to use, and is particularly attractive to creative types.

FIND YOUR BLOGGERS

Bloggers are some of the most important communicators on the Web, providing content that lingers for years and pops up quickly on search engines. Make a point of Googling the name of your company and the brand names of your products regularly, to see what people are saying about you in their blogs and any other online medium. When you find blogs that mention you, decide if a response would be appropriate—for example, if a customer had a good experience with your product but wishes it had one more feature, it may be worthwile to contact her. Most blogs have a comments section, which gives you a chance to connect directly with writers when they do not expect to hear from you. Make sure your comment comes as a pleasant surprise by thanking the blogger for whatever opinion she may have shared, and inviting her back to your business for another visit.

SO MANY BLOG SITES!

Once you start looking for blogs that mention your company, you may find that there are hundreds of such blog sites. Do you need to be concerned with every word someone writes about you? Focus on the blogs that come up in the first two or three pages of a Google search (or another search engine). The vast majority of readers will not go deeper than that, so if a dicey comment falls beyond this, chances are only a handful of the blogger's buddies will see it. Keep an eye out in your regular searches, however: Google's algorithms bring sites up to the top of the search if they're getting a lot of views, or "hits." This, in turn, brings them even more attention. If this happens to a blog post that mentions you, you will need to address the blogger's opinions by making contact.

LOOK FOR YOURSELF ON REDDIT

Who's following your news coverage? Reddit is a great place to find out. Users post links to all kinds of news they find interesting, so it's an easy place to determine if a story about your company is trending, or if there's something going on in your market sector that you need to see. Monitor this site to find out if people are commenting on stories about you; there's no real opportunity for your business to have a presence of its own here. Check out StumbleUpon and Digg as well, two more sites to which readers post links to news coverage.

STICK UP PHOTOS ON PINTEREST

People on Pinterest collect photos and videos, "pinning" them where they see them from any Internet connection and storing them here in collages of content. Your social media monitoring program should canvas this site for photos that pertain to your business. You can also build your own pages here with all the photos you like. This is a particularly good place to be if you have a wide variety of consumer products to sell, because you can post photos of them for others to find. For example, if you sell shoes, people may search for "red shoes," "red women's shoes," "red pumps," "red flats," and so on to find exactly what they are looking for, just as they would on Google. Here, however, they will find gorgeous photos of your shoes to compare to others. You can have a lot of fun with this site, while connecting with potential customers and answering lots of questions.

CHECK OUT POP CULTURE ON MYSPACE

Myspace is a social networking site with a strong emphasis on music (Justin Timberlake is part-owner). It was once the largest social networking site in the world . . . then along came Facebook. Now, however, young people are taking it back as their parents and grandparents grow fond of Facebook themselves. Those who want to know about pop culture come to Myspace. If fashion, food, drink, or music are your niche, this may be your spot. Although the number of users has decreased since its early days, those who hang out here may just represent your target demographic. You can also learn a lot from them about what's trending, what's on the verge of becoming hot, and what no longer is—just follow their conversations.

LOOK FOR FEEDBACK ON YELP

The ultimate consumer review site, Yelp is a great place to look for people who are happy or unhappy with your business: They will give you chapter and verse about their experience with you. Yelp includes reviews of pretty much every major city's restaurants, nightlife venues, retail businesses, and all other kinds of local services, making it the go-to site for this kind of detailed information. As a business, you will want to search for reviews here frequently. You can then respond to customers through the site's private messaging function, and discuss the reasons why they liked or didn't like your product or service. Be careful not to engage in arguments; if people don't want to connect with you, let it go.

FIND OUT WHAT CUSTOMERS ARE SAYING ON TRIPADVISOR

The premier review site of the travel industry, TripAdvisor carries reviews of hotels, restaurants, and attractions in every city and town in the world. If you run a business in any of these niches, you must monitor this site to see what people are saying about you. Many hoteliers and restaurant owners do this, and then post responses to reviews within hours—particularly if these reviews are not good, and they wish to apologize or better understand what went wrong. You can learn a great deal from the candid commentary here, and also get a chance to redeem yourself after a blunder by acknowledging a bad review and apologizing to your customer.

Choosing Social Media for Your Business

GO WHERE YOUR AUDIENCE IS

Not every business needs to be on Twitter or Facebook. It's hard to imagine what a company that sells sewer construction materials to municipalities would do with a Facebook page, much less a Twitter account. If you have a limited audience that you reach through specific channels, such as professional associations and unions, you may already be in contact with everyone in your industry. A Facebook page then becomes one more thing to manage . . . and it's likely to languish untouched, with few, if any, followers.

Know where your audience is and what kinds of communication will be most effective in reaching them. If you don't need to engage in social media, don't add it to your workload. But you should still use online monitoring tools to make sure the audience you thought was so small is not talking about you in places you did not expect.

REMIND CUSTOMERS ABOUT SECURITY

For the most part, live chat is not a secure platform. Make sure your customers know this if they are going to share confidential information with you. Give them an alternate, more secure way to provide such information, if that is in fact necessary to solve their problem.

LET CUSTOMERS KNOW ABOUT ANY WAITING TIME

If your customer must wait for a live chat, let him know where he is in the queue. Most people choose live chat because they have limited time and want help right away. If there are three people ahead of the customer, he may want to try back later when he has more time. Waiting in the proverbial dark will only make him frustrated with your system and your company.

USE ONLINE MONITORING TOOLS

New social media networks pop up seemingly overnight, so it's useful to utilize one or more of the tools available to see who's talking about your company and its products, and where.

Some of the most popular tools include Tweetdeck, which will monitor multiple Twitter accounts and perform automated searches on keywords and hashtags; TweetReach, a tool that can tell you how far your tweets travel and how much exposure they receive; and HowSociable, which tracks 12 social media sites, including WordPress, Tumblr, YouTube, LinkedIn, FourSquare, and Google+. (If you want Facebook, Twitter, and Pinterest, you have to pay extra.) Hootsuite, possibly the most widely used social media management app for business, lets you schedule tweets and postings in advance, and delivers analytics you can use to determine the true reach of your social media marketing.

WHY HAVE A FORUM?

Forums are places where like-minded people can share information. If your customers all come to your forum to talk to one another, you have the opportunity to watch the conversations closely and jump in with technical expertise and answers to questions about your products. This can make you the most responsive customer service organization in your market sector, which can help you build more business. When customers think about their next project and which companies have the expertise they need, yours will instantly come to mind.

USE PLAIN LANGUAGE, AND ASK ABOUT IT

It's easy in a live chat (or even on the phone) to start using a lot of technical jargon and numbers, just to move the conversation along and help customers more quickly. Some of them won't understand the jargon, however, so it's worth using as much plain language as possible until you have a sense of their comfort level with technical terms. Check with them by typing, "So far, is everything I've said clear? Please feel free to ask me about any terms you don't understand."

USE YOUR OWN FORUM TO COMMUNICATE WITH CUSTOMERS

Instead of turning to Facebook, Twitter, or one of a dozen or more other sites, many businesses may find it more beneficial to bring their target audience together on their own website.

Your webmaster can build a forum using off-the-shelf tools found online. Here, your customers can discuss issues of relevance to their business. You can monitor their exchanges and answer their questions, provide them with technical information, and encourage them to share their expertise.

Forum software packages include the free and open-source phpBB, IP.Board, and vBulletin, all of which are easy to use. Once you have a forum in place, you will need to invite your customers to participate and do some work to start and maintain conversations. Over time, your forums may grow on their own, as people in your customer base begin to tell one another that they're finding good information there.

BE CONSISTENT ACROSS CHANNELS

No matter how a customer contacts you for service—be it by phone, at your place of business, or online—the skill level of the customer service reps should be consistent. The fact that someone is providing online support through live chat, e-mail, or a forum should mean they are offering the same level of expertise and commitment to solving a problem as a person on the phone. Don't have an online rep suggest, "You really should call the company for that information." (The customer will ask, "Aren't you part of that company?")

POST TECHNICAL FAQS

In addition to the forums, maintain a list of the most frequently asked questions (FAQs) from customers, and post these in a searchable database on your website. Some of your clients may work at odd hours and need technical support when you are not available to help. If you can supply them with the information they need, they will remember that yours is the go-to site for fast answers to tricky issues.

The availability of technical information also relieves customers' stress, especially if they're the kind of people who don't like to ask for help.

POST SCHEMATICS AND OTHER ARCANE INFORMATION

If your business is in a highly technical field, chances are you have lots of technical specifications for your products or equipment. You may have schematics that show repair people how your equipment is built and the names of all of the parts. Perhaps you have technical manuals for your equipment or workstations. All of these documents—and probably hundreds more—exist as digital files, so you can easily turn them into PDFs for download from your website. The more of this information you make available for your customers, the more they will trust that their relationship with you has value.

MAKE SURE CUSTOMERS CAN SOLVE THE EASY PROBLEMS THEMSELVES

Thanks to search engines, self-help resources, technology affinity groups, and online forums, most customers can find the answers they need without picking up the phone to call you. This is good, because it saves them time and keeps them from sitting in hold queues at call centers. Make it as easy as possible for them to find what they need online, and they will recognize your great customer service even if you never have voice, live chat, or in-person contact with them.

IF IT'S LIVE CHAT, IT SHOULD BE PROMPT

How often have you clicked on the button that says, "Chat with a live person now!" and found that "now" means in about 10 minutes, when the live person becomes available? Worse, what about when the live chat is actually offline until the next morning? If you're going to offer live chat, you'll need a commitment that includes enough people to provide immediate access. This may be a daunting task if you have a wide base of customers, but the promptness and availability of help will pay off in loyalty and repeat business.

Dealing with the Public Online

PAY ATTENTION

You've seen brands melt down in social media channels, so you know the kind of damage social media can cause. The errors you don't see come from brands that spot them just as they start to emerge, and take care of them before they spread. Monitor social media carefully for mentions of your company—searching on keywords, setting alerts on your smartphone to let you know when you have new messages, and having Google Alerts show you when other media have brought you up.

SOCIAL MEDIA IS NOT FOR INTERNS

Your social media strategy—and yes, you should have one—is an integral part of the overall communications and marketing plan for your business. This means that your experienced, mature marketing and public relations people should be handling it. It's a fatal mistake to believe that social media is the purview of the young, and that seasoned minds should only be dealing with its "traditional" or "conventional" predecessors. Don't hand off the social media tasks to interns who have not yet developed the judgment required to avoid making snarky comments or posting questionable photos.

SET AND KEEP YOUR HOURS

It may not be a great move for a global, round-the-clock company like British Airways to tell its Twitter followers that it only responds to tweets during London business hours, but it's quite all right for a small florist in Des Moines, Iowa, to tell his customers he'll take their questions daily from 9 a.m. to 6 p.m. Let your customers know when they can expect to hear from you, so they don't think you're ignoring them.

EVERYONE HAS AN OPINION

The fact that someone flames your company for something you considered a minor issue does not have to become a crisis. In a Facebook page full of glowing reviews and comments from fans, one unhappy customer will not sink your business. Everyone has an opinion; there's no need to panic because someone has chosen to express a negative one. Respond politely to the customer in question, and ask if there is anything you can do to change her mind. The fact that you paid attention and strove for a reconciliation may just be enough to impress her and other readers of your page.

DON'T GET ANGRY

It goes without saying—though we'll say it anyway—that your interactions with customers and others online should *always* be cordial and professional. Don't be Amy's Baking Company, the Arizona eatery that got thrown off *Gordon Ramsay's Kitchen Nightmares* and then took their anger out on people who commented on their Facebook page. Vitriolic exchanges only make you look like a crazy person.

DON'T DELETE THE NEGATIVE COMMENT

You can delete things you don't like from your Facebook page, but that's a policy that will only get you into trouble. Customers and other visitors will quickly decide that you are censoring comments—a controversial practice at best. As long as the posting isn't inflammatory or blatantly untrue, it will soon be pushed down the page by other, largely more positive ones. Again, respond pleasantly and see if you can turn the writer's opinion with kindness and interest.

POST GUIDELINES FOR YOUR FACEBOOK PAGE

While the Internet is a place for free expression, you can still have some control over what you consider to be acceptable discourse on your company's Facebook page. Post some guidelines in your About section, indicating how you expect people to behave in terms of politeness, honesty, and integrity. Make it clear that you consider unacceptable behavior grounds for deletion of comments. When someone gets out of line, remove their post and send them a private message referring to these guidelines.

How to Mess Up Your Social Media

SNARK: THE CASE FOR AND AGAINST IT

Tesco Mobile, a British wireless communications company, is one of the few that can banter skillfully with people who disparage their service on Twitter. One famous exchange began when a young man named Jay Felipe tweeted, "Immediate turn off if a girl's mobile network is Tesco Mobile." Tesco's social media agency shot back with, "@JayFelipe Are you really in a position to be turning girls away?" The exchange escalated with great humor, and Tesco eventually sent Felipe a gift of soap, shampoo, hair gel, and a book on how to meet and woo women. Felipe's tweet with a photo of the gift: "Thank you @tescomobile for the gift much love to you!"

Tesco handled this with great skill, but most companies cannot match this kind of finesse, especially online. If you are tempted to play verbal games with your followers, get a second opinion. Check out your response to a snarky comment with coworkers or other people whose judgment you trust. If everyone laughs in appreciation, you may be safe. If not, don't engage. Sarcasm and snark can fall completely flat online.

NO ROBO-RESPONSES

When Kmart announced that it would be open on Thanksgiving Day 2013, it received a barrage of critical tweets about how its workers would not be able to spend the holiday with their families. Kmart had clearly decided in advance to use one response to all of them: "Kmart is staffing w/ teams & seasonal associates when possible, giving them opportunity to make extra money during holiday." This canned response appeared over and over again as the company's social media team posted it to every individual critic's feed. This resulted in hundreds of identical messages—a total fail for an already shaky image.

Even if you get thousands of tweets, resist the urge to use this kind of robotic response. It's better to address the whole world with a single line than to respond to thousands of tweets in exactly the same way, over and over again.

GUARD YOUR PASSWORDS

Be careful with your social media accounts and with your choice of those who administer them. Access to social media has been known to backfire on companies during times of internal crisis, especially if employees with passwords are fired or laid off. HMV, a British entertainment company, saw the error in its ways when its social media team blasted its Twitter account during a purge of corporate offices. "We're tweeting live from HR where we're all being fired! Exciting!" one suddenly ex-employee told the Twitter universe.

TRY NOT TO BE TONE-DEAF

One of the most tragic—and yet, one of the funniest—Twitter failures of all time took place in November 2013, when J.P. Morgan Chase Vice Chairman Jimmy Lee decided to hold a question-and-answer session on his feed. People began tweeting their questions almost immediately, and most of them took this tone: "How far do you and your financial sector gang members think you can push things before you are driven off the continent?" Another non-fan tweeted, "When will you all go to jail?" Hundreds of questions like these crowded the Chase hashtag #AskJPM until Lee canceled the scheduled Q&A.

It seems impossible that a multinational bank once embroiled in the 2008 banking crisis would be so tone-deaf that they would have no idea how this might turn into a nightmare. Here's what we can learn: It doesn't matter if you like or dislike the way the general public feels about your company. They feel what they feel, and their opinions must become part of your full strategy of two-way communication with them.

How Others Can Mess Up Your Social Media

NIP THE PROBLEM IN THE BUD

In previous parts, we've talked about dealing with angry customers on the spot, both in person and over the phone. Resolving their issues quietly and immediately will likely keep them from doing the thing that can hurt you the most: talking trash about you online.

In the digital age, one angry tweet or Facebook post can attract many views, turning public opinion against you and making it very difficult for you to turn things around. Even if the writer's perception of the incident is completely wrong, it can spread through the social media universe within hours— especially if it includes video.

Your first preventive measure should be to solve an angry customer's issue in person whenever you can. If you manage to do this, chances are she won't tweet or post about it at all.

USE SNOPES

Snopes.com is one of the greatest rumor-debunking sites on the Web. The Snopes staff seeks out every urban legend and every tale that doesn't pass the smell test, and tracks down the origin of the story, and whatever truth there is to it. Millions of people go to Snopes before they repost anything that seems too fishy to be real. Send Snopes the libelous tweet and ask them to debunk it and post their results.

HOW TO GET A VIDEO REMOVED FROM FACEBOOK

Once the video is online, you will have to do some work to remove it.

If the video is on Facebook, find it and click on it to expand it. Go to the Options menu on the bottom right and click Report Video.

If you can't see the video yourself, you can still report it by submitting an Intellectual Property Infringement Form. To find this form, pull down the menu under the arrow at the far right of the Facebook screen, and go to Report a Problem. Click on Abusive Content, and then Something I Can't See. Follow the instructions.

WHEN THE TWEET IS OUT THERE

A customer left your establishment with a problem you could not solve, and then tweeted about it to his friends. He included your Twitter handle in the message so you could see what he had done, because he wants you to know he's getting his revenge.

What do you do? First, write him the most conciliatory tweet you can muster. Make it something like this: "@JohnSmythe, we are truly sorry for the inconvenience. Please give us another chance to help. DM with your phone; let's talk." DM means direct message; you've asked him to send you a private message with his contact information.

Now John has the ball; he can toss it back to you by messaging you with his phone number, or he can run with it and continue to trash you. Be absolutely courteous and polite in your replies—even when he tries to bait you into a fight. After a while, he will start to look foolish, and his anger will lose steam.

PREPARE YOUR CUSTOMER SERVICE PEOPLE

If you're in the midst of a public relations crisis, your customer service staff will be on the front lines. They will get many calls from customers and other members of the public, and will need to know exactly what to say.

Prepare a question-and-answer document that provides clear, truthful responses to the questions you expect to receive (and do your best to think about others that might not come immediately to mind). Remember that there may be questions you would prefer not to answer, but that the public expects you to answer anyway. This is not the time to finesse or dodge. The more prepared your customer service employees are for the onslaught, the better they can give sincere responses to anxious or angry customers . . . and the better your company will weather the storm.

SEND AN E-MAIL TO YOUR CUSTOMERS

Explain to your clients that you know about the tweet and its widespread impact, and that you want them to know the facts—then list these in the most concise and unemotional way you can. Provide a basic outline of the steps you're taking to quell the rumor. Finally, thank them for their continued patronage and offer to answer any questions they may have. Give them an easy way to reach you personally (via phone or e-mail) if your customer base is relatively small—otherwise, direct them to your customer service line and make sure it is well-staffed.

USE TWITTER TO BEAT THE TWEET

You can search for keywords on Twitter to find all the retweets of the original message, and answer every single one of them with a link to the statement on your website. Later, when you have positive media stories, you can go back and post links to those as well.

THE INCRIMINATING VIDEO

If you are unlucky enough that your angry customer has unflattering video footage of something or someone at your company—an employee who lost his temper, a manager who let a sarcastic comment slip, or a gatekeeper who said something bigoted or insensitive—you may have to take dramatic action.

You are much better served by refusing to talk to customers who come in with a GoPro camera or who hold up a smartphone and start recording your conversation. Tell them, "Please put the camera down, and we can talk. I won't talk to you on camera." You have a right to do this; any person can refuse to be photographed or recorded on video. If they persist, keep saying, "I will be happy to talk to you and solve your problem, but I'm asking you not to videotape this." Do not lose your temper or become in any way aggressive—don't give them a great video to post.

Some customers will get a video recording no matter what you say, and the ones who are most angry with you will post it online. They may also post the video of you asking not to be videotaped, as if the act of refusing to be recorded could make you look bad. Every situation is different, of course, but if you smile and manage not to get angry, the person making the video will generally appear foolish for trying to record you.

LIES, DAMNED LIES, AND TWEETS: FACING DOWN LIBEL

Imagine your company makes windmills, and you're about to build a wind farm on land owned by the local county. Someone in the community, however, doesn't want to face this "eyesore" from his window, so he starts tweeting about your company's windmills. At first his tweets are about how ugly they are and how wind power isn't any cheaper or more efficient than coal-fired power. You can refute these things, but the deal is done and you don't really want to engage with this person.

Then one day he posts a tweet saying your windmills have killed more than one million birds in the past year. He has no proof of this, and you know for a fact it's not true, but now you have a problem. What do you do?

You're dealing with libel, the deliberate publication of a false statement that is damaging to your company's reputation. Now your discourse with this person is a legal matter, and you need to take legal action. Law moves slowly, however, so this false statement will remain in the public eye until your attorney can get it removed.

You can take action on your own immediately. Approach the tweeter, let him know that you've seen the tweet, you know it to be untrue, and you are asking him to take it down. If he refuses, you can have your attorney write a letter stating that legal action will follow.

In most cases, this will work. The tweeter knows he hasn't got a legal leg to stand on, so he may simply remove the tweets.

HOW TO GET A VIDEO REMOVED FROM INSTAGRAM

If you have been tagged in the video—in other words, if the person who posted the video identified you in it—reporting it is fairly easy. From the Photo of Me menu below the post, choose Report Inappropriate.

If you have not been tagged, you may not be able to see the video. However, you can still report it. Go to help.instagram.com, choose Privacy & Safety Center from the menu on the left, and then choose Report Something. You'll get another menu, from which you can choose Abuse & Spam. At the bottom of the page, you'll find a link from which you can send a report on something you can't actually see. You will need to provide the name and contact information of the person who posted the video.

HOW TO GET A VIDEO REMOVED FROM YOUTUBE

If your angry customer posted a video to YouTube, you will be able to view it easily—but so will just about everyone else in the entire world. YouTube does not require people to have an account or be connected to anyone else in order to view content. Viewers can link the video to their websites, and media can upload it into stories about you.

You can report the video quickly and easily. Below the video player, click on the More button. On the drop-down menu, click Report. Choose a reason for flagging the video, and provide additional details in the box provided. It could take some time before the video comes down, and it's possible that YouTube staff will decide the video deserves to remain in place.

DAMAGE CONTROL

Removing a video is at the discretion (read: mercy) of the social media sites on which it has been posted. If it is not obscene and doesn't put you or anyone else in danger, it may not come down at all.

What you do next depends on the video's content. If it shows that the customer who uploaded it had a legitimate issue, and that it was handled poorly by one or more of your company's employees, your best move is for management to contact her directly and resolve it to her satisfaction. The more publicity her video gets, the more your company will have to do to appease her.

While you negotiate with her, you will also have to decide what to do with the employee(s) in the video. Did they handle the situation to the best of their abilities? If not, you may have no choice but to take disciplinary action.

There is no easy way out once a bad exchange has made it onto the Internet. Your next steps will be painful for your company and the people involved, so get them over with as quickly as possible and begin to move past the incident.

MEANWHILE, DON'T FORGET YOUR CUSTOMERS

Before going to the media about the libelous tweet, you need to reach out to your customers to let them know it's untrue—don't take it for granted that they already know. Indeed, if the runaway tweet has reached them, they may be having second thoughts about wind power in general and your company in particular. Don't let that happen.

HOW TO STOP THE LIE

If the Twitter-verse is abuzz with a fabricated accusation, it's time to move away from social media solutions and use another tool for disseminating information: traditional media. You may have been hoping beyond hope that you could keep this entire affair from them, but, if you want to put it to rest, you may have to recruit their help.

Be the first to make contact with them. Tell your whole story before they find the libelous tweeter. You want the media message to be, "A runaway tweet tells a lie about a local company," not, "Can a tweeter's story about a local company be true?"

If you have never dealt with the media before and don't know what to say to turn this story around, enlist the help of a public relations firm. You only have one chance to get this right, so use professionals who can make it happen for you.

HOW TO GET A VIDEO REMOVED FROM TWITTER

Go to support.twitter.com/forms/abusiveuser and fill out the form you find there. You will need the URL (web address) of the tweet containing the video, and the username of the person who posted it.

There's no indication on the form of how long it will take the Twitter staff to view the tweet with the video and determine if it meets their criteria for removal. For the record, these criteria include offensive or disrespectful content, harassment, specific violent threats involving physical safety, exposed private information, or spam. You will need to make a cogent case that the video is harming you or your company to convince Twitter to remove it.

GET AHEAD OF AN INTERNET LIE

How long did these steps take—a day, maybe two? In that time, one hundred people who agree with the tweeter have already retweeted his message. Those one hundred people each have two hundred followers, many of whom retweet the message as well, so another two hundred people see each retweet. In the space of an hour or so, thousands of people have viewed this message. The original tweeter is just a username to them, so they have no way to disconfirm the veracity of his statement. They just take it as fact.

The original tweet may be gone, but it's been duplicated so many times that it no longer matters. It has gone viral, spreading through the Twitter system the way the flu spreads through the human body.

What do you do? Here's the painful truth: You can't stop a tweet that's gone viral. Your best move is to neutralize its impact as quickly as you can.

It's time to get your facts into the conversation. Where did the original tweeter get his information? Did it come from another company whose windmills don't have the bird safeguards that yours do? Talk about that. What other facts have you got? Tweet these, and also get them on your Facebook page. Trump the liar's message with your own.

POST A STATEMENT ON YOUR WEBSITE

Work with your communications staff or public relations advisors on a statement that explains why the tweet is not true, adding that you're prepared to take legal action if necessary. Post this statement right on your site's landing page, so that all visitors will see it immediately.

HAVE A PR CRISIS PLAN

Every business needs a PR crisis plan—a list of steps you'll take to deal with online misinformation and keep it from growing to a point where it can jeopardize your work. It's worth the exercise to put this together, using the steps suggested here and others that might be appropriate to your line of business. Your document should include a list of team members who will execute the plan, and also stipulate who will be in charge and what they'll be expected to do. This will help you keep the crisis from becoming too disruptive to your daily work—which is what ultimately keeps your business afloat. (It will also keep employees from giving their two cents on what the best course of action might be, a practice that can bog down communication at a time in which speed is key.)

SWIFT JUSTICE

When members of the Sigma Alpha Epsilon fraternity at the University of Oklahoma were recorded singing a racist song about lynching black students, university authorities dealt swift justice. President David Boren expelled the two students who had led the chant and dismissed the whole fraternity from campus, giving members until midnight of the day on which the video emerged to pack up and vacate the house. While legal scholars have argued that the students had a constitutional right to sing this song, the president's reaction—which came quickly and without hesitation—was widely regarded as an appropriate move. Had University of Oklahoma waffled on its response, it may have come across as a racist institution—a label that could have had lasting ramifications and triggered a much larger national discussion. When an unquestionable wrong has been committed, move swiftly to make it right.

Going Viral

YOU CAN'T DELIBERATELY MAKE SOMETHING GO VIRAL

A virus, by definition, is self-propelling. If a company tries to force a video or photo to go viral, it's almost certain to fizzle out. You've probably seen a couple of these attempts: a hashtag promoted in a TV commercial to get everyone on Twitter talking about some product, or a photo so deliberately silly no one thinks it's spontaneous. These things won't go viral because they don't capture people's imagination.

If someone stands in the lobby of your fast food restaurant and calls out, "Okay, I'm going to post this on Twitter and show everyone what you're doing here, and it's going to go viral," they are either dreaming or bluffing. No one has control over what goes viral and what does not.

CONTENT IS KING

If someone with a smartphone actually catches your employees spitting on the hamburgers, you can bet your last dollar that it's going to go viral. That's just the kind of image that will kindle the interest of millions of people, especially if you happen to own a franchise of a multinational chain.

The key to keeping any videos of this restaurant (or any business) from going viral is to give the person with the smartphone nothing of interest to shoot. Run a good business, do good work, and serve a good product, and you won't find yourself and your employees featured on *Tosh 2.0* or trending on Twitter.

THE VIRAL MESSAGE CYCLE, AND HOW YOU CAN RESPOND

It starts with someone posting something on Facebook, or Instagram, or YouTube, or the like. His post draws the attention of two other people, who then decide to repost it. All of these people's followers see their reposts, and a handful of them go ahead and share them as well. Now hundreds more can see the original content, and soon a large crowd is discussing it. In a day or so, an innocuous thing has turned into a national sensation, and the media picks it up. By now, some people are calling it stupid; others are fascinated and keep the conversation going. Finally, someone at the beginning of the information stream notes that the content has been manipulated, thus deflating all the speculation and ending the discussion. The frenzy is over, and the world moves on to the next viral tidbit.

Many companies make the mistake of trying to wait out the frenzy without taking action. If you're riding a wave of positive publicity, there may be no need to respond; just enjoy the fun and watch to see if those feelings change. If the publicity is bad, however—for example, if an employee has been caught on video doing something nasty—you need to respond right away. Announce that you're looking into the situation and plan to resolve it swiftly, and then do so. The resolution may not be fun for you, but an angry public will only make the crisis worse.

WHAT IS YOUR VIRAL MESSAGE STRATEGY?

A message, photo, or video becomes viral when it is reposted and retweeted by so many people that just about everyone knows about it. Often aided by media coverage of one kind or another—whether via CNN, the Huffington Post, or Comedy Central's @Midnight—the material becomes a sensation because it's particularly funny, horrifying, weird, quirky, baffling, or heartwarming. Viral messages almost always elicit a strong reaction, be it positive or negative.

If you're the one who posted the original video hoping it would go viral, you're a winner. But if the video is somehow about you or your company and it puts you in a bad light, you've got a problem on your hands. Don't wait until you're in the thick of it to put together a defensive strategy; you must think through in advance how you'll handle a situation like this, when you can calmly and clearly decide who should be in charge, what steps you should take, and how you should move beyond the negative publicity.

PART

50 THINGS NEVER
TO DO OR SAY

When a customer insults you, raises his or her voice, uses profanity, or threatens to have you fired, it makes you angry as well—and you may be tempted to match her tone and manner. This is only natural, of course, but it's not a good way to demonstrate excellent service.

The examples in this part of the book will help you find your way past an impulsive reaction to this type of situation, and on to a solution that works for both your company and your client. While every customer interaction is different, these scenarios will help you learn what kinds of reactions to avoid, and what not to say if you want to defuse a difficult moment.

They have all been compiled from real accounts of abysmal customer service in restaurants, stores, call centers, and all kinds of other businesses. The perpetrators were thoughtless employees who said the first thing that popped into their heads, thus insulting or offending their clients and probably losing their business forever.

If the customer service people quoted in the Wrong categories below make you gasp, roll your eyes, or shake your head in disbelief, remember the Right quotes when you're dealing with your own customers. You'll be glad you took the high road, no matter how tough it gets.

DON'T
IGNORE
SOMEONE WAITING

You are a pharmacy assistant, and a customer comes to the counter just as you're working out a complicated health insurance problem at your workstation. When you don't look up right away, she says, "Excuse me . . ."

WRONG: Don't make any eye contact with the customer, in hopes that she will go away. Keep your eyes on the screen, frown, and say, "Just hold on, I'll get to you when I can."

RIGHT: Look up and smile. Say, "I'll be happy to help you in just a moment. I'm in the middle of a tricky health insurance issue for a customer. If you have other shopping to do, maybe you'd like to go ahead and do that? Then I'll ring up everything for you right here."

DON'T
INTERROGATE
your customer

You work in a store that sells electronics and small parts for electronic projects. A customer comes in with an odd request for a part that you sell, but that most people wouldn't use. You'd really like to know more about what it can do.

WRONG: Ask the customer, "You want what? Why would you want that? No one ever asks for that part. Are you sure that's what you want?"

RIGHT: "Wow, interesting. We have that in stock—let me grab one for you. We don't get a lot of requests for that. Would you mind if I asked what you're going to do with it? It would be a good thing for me to know, the next time someone comes in for one."

DON'T FORGET *to* COMMUNICATE *any changes*

You work in a call center for a company that makes gift packages of fruits, sweets, and savory goodies. A customer calls, and he's very angry. He's trying to track down a package for which he paid a steep premium for overnight delivery. It's been a week, and the package has not yet arrived. You look up the order number and discover that the item is on backorder, so it still has not shipped. The customer was never notified that it was not available.

WRONG: "Well, it never went out. It's on backorder. I don't know what to tell you, but there's nothing I can do for you. You probably should have chosen something else."

RIGHT: "I am so sorry for this, sir, but the item has not yet shipped. It turns out that this specific item is backordered. I don't have an explanation for why you were not informed of this. First, I will refund the cost of overnight delivery to your credit card right now. Second, if you are willing to choose a different item that's in stock, we will get that out today, with no charge for the shipping. I also want to offer you a free gift for yourself as our apology for your inconvenience."

DON'T TURN DISAPPOINTMENT *into* FRUSTRATION

You are the customer service representative for an upscale furniture store. A customer who has spent more than $5,000 with your store calls with a problem. The dining room table she just received has been stained a much darker shade than she anticipated, and it doesn't match the rest of the furniture. Easter Sunday is in three days, and she wanted to have the table for the holiday dinner, to seat her whole family.

WRONG: "Well, I'm looking at the order, and it says the table is the same shade as the rest of your furniture. I don't know what to tell you. I can't come out and look at it, but if you're returning it, we'd have to come and pick it up this afternoon. You can't have it both ways—you either want the table or you don't. I guess you'll have to get some trays for Easter dinner."

RIGHT: "Let me send out a technician this afternoon to take a look at the color and see what's up. If it's the wrong color, we can arrange to pick it up from you on Monday, after the holiday. I'll just ask you to use a table pad and a tablecloth to protect the finish."

DON'T DENY
RESPONSIBILITY

You work in a call center for a technology company. You receive a call from a customer who has just bought a piece of your equipment, and when he plugs it into the network and powers it up, the whole network freezes. It's your job to figure out what's going on.

WRONG: "Well, it's not supposed to do that, so you must have done something to it. In other words, it's your fault. You must have screwed this up somehow."

RIGHT: "That must be really frustrating. Our product should be entirely compatible with your system, so there must be an issue in there somewhere. Let's start at the beginning and work our way through the network."

DON'T
SWEAR
(obviously)

You're still the technical service person in the call center described above. When the customer becomes angry because you told him the problem was his fault, he demands to speak with your supervisor.

WRONG: You say, "F*** you!" or "You must be sh**ting me," or anything remotely similar.

RIGHT: "My supervisor will be with you in a moment. May I place you on hold for a few minutes until she's available?" (Then place him on hold.)

DON'T LOSE *your* PATIENCE

You work in a call center for a cable company. A customer calls for information about the channels in each of the packages, and why some seem to have the same channels at a higher price. You try to explain, but he just doesn't seem to get it.

WRONG: "Look, I've explained this over and over. I can't make it any clearer."

RIGHT: "I know this all sounds really complicated. I'll tell you what—do you have Internet access? Let's both go to the page on the website, where this is all spelled out to help our customers understand it. I can take you through it and see if I can make it clearer for you."

DON'T SHAME
the ELDERLY

You work in the patient information center for a health insurance provider. A customer calls with questions about which insurance to buy as a supplement to Medicare. She sounds elderly, and she doesn't seem to hear everything you say.

WRONG: "I've already said that three times. Do you have your hearing aids in? I can't sit here and shout into the phone. This is all on the website anyway—if you can't hear, go look at it there."

RIGHT: "Ma'am, I'm sorry that I'm not making myself clear. This is a very complicated topic, and it can be hard to understand. What was the last thing I said that made sense to you? Let me start again from there, and we'll take it a step at a time."

DON'T EXPECT
your customers to
KNOW
YOUR INTERNAL PROCESSES

Your plumbing parts company has a process that customers need to follow to return unused products. A client calls with a list of products he would like to return. He wants to come over and bring all of his returns with him, but he doesn't have a return merchandise authorization number.

WRONG: "If you followed our process, you'd have the number. There's nothing I can do for you without it. Go to our website and follow the process."

RIGHT: "Sure, come on over, and we can fill out the paperwork right here. It only takes a few minutes. If you would prefer to have the RMA before you get here, I can give you the web address for the form."

DON'T
MICROMANAGE
your patrons

You work in a bakery that offers free samples of some of your many tasty creations. A plump customer comes in and asks to try the blueberry cheese breakfast bread.

WRONG: "Do you really think you should be eating that? It wouldn't hurt you to take some weight off." (Yes, this actually happens, and more often than you might think.)

RIGHT: "Certainly. That's one of my favorites. Here's a sample. Is there anything else you'd like to try?"

DON'T REFUSE *to* BEND THE RULES

You work in a clothing store, and a customer who bought a necklace a few days ago comes back with it in pieces. It's a necklace with many tiny strands, and several of them have snapped. The customer freely admits that she snagged it on a sweater. She's hoping you will exchange the necklace and send this one back to the manufacturer.

WRONG: "If it's your fault, I can't take the necklace back. That's our policy—no returns on that necklace. You should have seen how fragile it was before you decided to buy it."

RIGHT: "Oh, that's so disappointing. Of course we'll exchange it. Would you mind if I give you a few tips about how to wear it? These necklaces are so fragile that you need to do some things to keep the strands from getting caught."

DON'T BE INSENSITIVE
to PEOPLE *with* DISABILITIES

You are the host in a restaurant. A customer comes in who has difficulty speaking, and you can't tell exactly why. He seems to have a physical disability of some kind, though he does not use a walker or wheelchair.

WRONG: You assume he's drunk. You turn up your nose and walk away without greeting him.

RIGHT: You make eye contact, smile, and say, "Good evening, sir, how can I help you?" If he has difficulty speaking, continue to make eye contact and wait patiently for him to tell you the number of people in his party or anything else he needs to say.

DON'T REFUSE *to* SOLVE PROBLEMS

You work at the technical support counter in a large electronics store. A customer comes over with a laptop and a receipt that shows she bought it yesterday. She says it won't power up, no matter what she does.

WRONG: "Well, if it won't power up, I can't do anything. It has to be on and working for me to troubleshoot it. What did you do to it after you left here yesterday? Did you drop it?"

RIGHT: "I'm so sorry for the inconvenience. Let's walk over to customer service, and you can exchange this laptop for one that works. We'll take it out of the box and make sure it's working before you leave."

DON'T DISMISS
a Genuine
CONCERN

You work for an insurance company. A customer calls about damage to his house because of flooding that took place in the spring, when the snow from an unusually hard winter melted and the water seeped into his basement. It turns out he did not purchase a flood rider with his homeowner's insurance.

WRONG: "Look, this is your problem, not ours. You should have bought flood insurance. I can't do anything for you."

RIGHT: "I am so sorry, but you are not covered in full for this flooding. However, there may be parts of the damage that are covered by your insurance. First, let's see what we can do to help you get past this incident. Then, before we hang up, I want to be sure you're covered for the next time something like this happens. I can give you some pricing on a flood rider, and you can call back when you've had a little time to think about what you'd like to do."

DON'T HIDE BEHIND *a* HIGHER AUTHORITY

You work in a pharmacy, and one of your customers calls with a refill for a medication he has been taking for some time. The pharmacist notices for the first time that this medicine duplicates another one the customer has also been taking for years, so he refuses to fill the prescription, citing rules from the insurance companies. The customer becomes angry at this, because his doctor wants him to be on both. He describes the symptoms he will have if he's not.

WRONG: "Well, the pharmacist says no. What do you want me to do about it? If your symptoms are so bad, you should see a doctor about that."

RIGHT: "The pharmacist has to do what he feels is right, but let's see if we can get this sorted out. We can call your doctor's office right now and have him explain this to our pharmacist. I'm so sorry for the inconvenience, but if we can't reach the doctor right away, you may have to come back for your prescription. Again, I apologize for all of this."

DON'T MAKE
A CUSTOMER'S LOSS
HARDER
than it needs to be

You work for an insurance company. A customer calls and says she is the executor of an estate, and she is calling to cancel her mother's car insurance account.

WRONG: "Well, we need to speak to your mother." When the customer repeats that her mother is dead: "Then there's nothing we can do without her authorization. Your best bet is to close her checking account so we can't take out any more automatic payments."

RIGHT: "I am very sorry for your loss. I just need a copy of the death certificate to close the account. Let me give you a fax number, so you can fax that to us with her account number on the cover sheet."

DON'T EVER
ACCUSE
your customer of
LYING

You work in a wireless service provider's retail store. A customer comes in with a smartphone that appears perfectly fine on the outside, but has stopped working altogether. The customer says it's fully charged. He says he was using it normally when it just went dead.

WRONG: "You must have done something to it—dropped it or something. I can't tell what you did, but this has got to be your fault."

RIGHT: "There are some things we can try to see what the problem is, but if we can't fix it, let's look at your contract and see what we can do to get you back online today."

DON'T COVER
for YOUR
COMPANY'S
ERROR

You work for a company that makes software for use in an industrial setting. A customer calls about a problem with his software. After a few minutes of listening to his description, you duplicate the problem perfectly. It's obviously a software bug.

WRONG: "The software is working as designed. There's really nothing I can do about this until we bring out the next version."

RIGHT: "Thank you so much for bringing this to our attention. I'm going to report this bug to our software engineers right now and see if we can get a quick fix for you. If not, we'll see if there's a workaround for the time being. I'm sorry for the inconvenience, but I really appreciate you coming to us with this."

DON'T
FAT-SHAME

---

*You work part-time in a women's clothing store while you put
yourself through college. You are young and thin, while many of
your customers are older and curvier. A customer comes in looking for a special dress for a wedding she's attending. The dresses
she tries on are a little tight, particularly around the bust line.*

WRONG: "You should get some Spanx and support pantyhose,
and one of those bras that pulls in all the excess."

RIGHT: "That looks really uncomfortable, especially for a nice
event like a wedding. The next size up will be more flattering,
and you will look more confident and at ease. Would you like
to try it?"

DON'T GET
DEFENSIVE
about small things

You work in a store, and when you ring up a customer's items, he stops you. He points out that the sign on the shelf says the price of an item is $2 less than its price on the register.

WRONG: "That's how it rings up. You can go back there and look for yourself, or bring me the sign from the shelf with the product number on it."

RIGHT: "Let me get someone to check that for you. If you're right, you certainly should save some money."

DON'T DENY ERRORS

You work in a store, and a customer comes in with an item she purchased the day before. She was charged $2 more for the item than the marked-down amount on the tag. She happens to be a customer you waited on yesterday.

WRONG: "That was the register's fault, not mine. I can't do anything about it."

RIGHT: "Thank you for straightening this out; I'm sorry you had to come all the way back here. Here is your refund."

DON'T GET IN THE WAY

You work in a call center. You receive a call from a customer, and he immediately asks to be transferred to another rep. He says he just spent two hours on the phone with her, and then got disconnected accidentally. He has his incident number and other information to help you find her quickly.

WRONG: "Thank you for calling ABC Software. I would be happy to help you find that representative. First, may I have your name and the serial number of your product? Thank you very much for that information. Now, I will check your contact information. Are you living at 235 Riverside Avenue in Dubuque, Iowa? Thank you very much for that information. I have your phone number as 555-555-2345, is that correct? Thank you very much. And your e-mail address is burningman@gmail.com, correct? Can you describe for me the problem you are having with your software? Sir, please stop screaming so I can hear you better."

RIGHT: "Okay, I see that you were talking to Denise. If you get disconnected again, her direct line is 877-444-1223. I'll transfer you now."

DON'T DISMISS
OTHERS' PLANS

You work at an event supply company. A customer contacts you to ask for an estimate on her event, which is eight weeks away. She gives you an itemized list of equipment and supplies, and tells you she needs the estimate by a specific date three weeks from now. Three weeks later, on the morning of the deadline, she calls to find out why she has not received it.

WRONG: "The person who took the information is on vacation, and she didn't leave any information about this. What's your real, drop-dead deadline? I don't really want to have to go through the whole list with you again."

RIGHT: "I am terribly sorry for the oversight. I can't say exactly where the disconnection happened here, but let's go ahead and make sure you have what you need. If you don't mind going through the list with me again, I will take care of the estimate today."

DON'T DENY CREDITS *or* REFUNDS

when the issue is your fault

You work for a telephone company. Your company had a system-wide outage and customers were without service for two days. You receive a call from a client who demands a credit for the lost service.

WRONG: "We can't give everyone a credit for this. Do you have any idea what that would cost us?"

RIGHT: "Of course we will credit you, sir. Again, we apologize for the inconvenience to you. You'll see the credit on your next bill."

DON'T
make the customer
FEEL LIKE A
DEADBEAT

You work for a credit card company. A customer calls about a late payment charge on his bill. He says he never received a bill in the previous month, so he didn't pay. He says he believes this is your company's error.

WRONG: "You are responsible for paying your bill, regardless of whether you receive it or not. You can go online and see your bill. What are you, an idiot?"

RIGHT: "Miss, I am sorry for the inconvenience. It is the policy of all credit card companies that customers are responsible for paying their bills on time, even if you don't receive the bill. I would like to help you, though, and also make sure that you receive all of your bills from us in the future. First, I can give you a one-time credit for the late fee. We can also go into your account online and make sure that you get e-mail alerts when your bill is ready, so you can look at the bill online. Do you have access to a computer and the Internet right now?"

DON'T MAKE FALSE ACCUSATIONS

You work for a credit card company. A customer calls with a mystery charge on her bill—a transaction she says is not hers.

WRONG: "You say that's not your charge, but we will need to investigate further. If it turns out to be your charge after all, that's fraud—and you'll pay a penalty. Is that really what you want?"

RIGHT: "Thank you very much for reporting this. Do you have the credit card in your possession now? If it's been lost, I can connect you with the department that will cancel the card for your protection, and send you a new card. If you have the card, I can take the information about the charge, and we can research it. We will keep you informed of our progress by regular mail."

DON'T
ESCALATE

A customer calls your company and begins to shout at you almost from the moment you pick up the phone.

WRONG: "I can't help you when you're yelling at me. You're not listening to me. Stop yelling, or I'll end this call and you won't get anything from us!"

RIGHT: "Sir, I want to help you. I'm glad you called us, and I want to be sure this gets resolved. I didn't catch all of what you were saying. Could I ask you to start at the beginning, so I can take notes and understand the whole problem?"

DON'T SAY "I DON'T KNOW"

A customer shopping in your store has a question about a product. She asks about the material from which a particular suit is made.

WRONG: "Oh, I have no idea."

RIGHT: "That's a good question. I don't know that off the top of my head, but let me check on what the manufacturer says about this suit."

DON'T TREAT
the customer
LIKE AN
IMBECILE

You work at the service desk in an automobile dealership. A customer comes in with his car, and he is absolutely certain the problem he's having is with a particular part. However, his car is fairly new, and the part he thinks is the problem is not even used anymore.

WRONG: "Are you kidding? They haven't put that part in cars since 1992. How can you not know that?"

RIGHT: "That's interesting, sir, but the symptoms you describe could be caused by a number of things. Let us take a look, and we'll call you as soon as we know what the trouble is. In the meantime, will you need a loaner car today? We have one available for you."

DON'T STICK TO POLICY
as if it's
CARVED IN STONE

A customer buys an item from your store during a clearance sale, when every purchase is marked as final. Two days later, he returns and shows you some strange marks on the product that he did not see before. He wants to return the item.

WRONG: "Everything was labeled final. That's the way it is. You should have looked more closely at the item before you bought it. And how can I know that you didn't take it home and get those marks on it yourself?"

RIGHT: "Sir, our policy is that all sales are final, but I want to make it right for you. I would be happy to exchange this item for a similar one of equal value. Please take a look around and see what you like."

DON'T TELL A CUSTOMER *to* "CALM DOWN"

You get a call from an irate customer. He has a legitimate problem, but he's very angry about it and shouts at you.

WRONG: "Calm down. I won't talk to you if you're hollering at me."

RIGHT: Let the customer finish. There's no point in trying to stop him; he needs to shout himself out. Then say, "Sir, I'm terribly sorry for the inconvenience. I want to remedy this situation, so let's start at the beginning again."

DON'T BE LAZY

You work in a store, and a customer comes up to you and asks about a specific product. You're fairly certain it's in stock.

WRONG: "Did you look for it? It should be right over there" (pointing vaguely).

RIGHT: "I believe that's in stock. Let me take you to it. If it's not there, I'll see if we have more in the back."

DON'T BE
VINDICTIVE

You own a consignment shop. A customer comes in with an evening gown she'd like to have you sell. You usually require appointments for this.

WRONG: "We only look at clothing for consignment between 2 p.m. and 4 p.m. on Tuesdays. You'll have to come back then."

RIGHT: "I'd be happy to take a look at your gown. Just for future reference, we normally ask people to call for appointments for this. So if you have any suits or other clothing you'd like us to sell, give me a call so I can be sure I'm available for you when you come in."

DON'T
act as if
YOU'RE
BETTER

You own a consignment shop, and a customer brings you some suits to sell. The suits look at little dusty, as if they've been in the closet a long time.

WRONG: "Why would you bring something in here that's not clean and in perfect condition? I have to maintain my reputation for quality."

RIGHT: "These are very nice suits, and I would like to sell them. Let me get a clothing brush, so we can see if this is dust or fading around the shoulders. If it turns out to be fading, I can recommend some other places where you can take them."

DON'T TURN AWAY A CUSTOMER

for not following your rules

A customer comes to your store just as you're about to lock the doors for the night.

WRONG: "We're closing now. Come back tomorrow."

RIGHT: "Is there something I can help you with quickly? Our hours are 9 a.m. to 9:30 p.m., but I'll be happy to help you now if you know what you need."

DON'T DENY HELP

You work in a large hardware store. A customer comes into your department and asks a question about something in another department.

WRONG: "Lady, this is the electrical department. You need to go to the paint department."

RIGHT: "I'm not the best person to ask about that—my expertise is in electrical. Let's go over to the paint department and see if someone there can help you."

DON'T
behave like a
SCHOOLMASTER

A customer in your store asks you to get something down for her from a high shelf.

WRONG: "What do you say . . . ?" (waiting for the customer to say "please").

RIGHT: "Certainly, I'll be happy to help you with that. I'll go get the rolling stairs and be right back."

DON'T PUT THE RESPONSIBILITY *on others*

A customer asks for an item that's not on the shelf. You discover the store has run out of that item.

WRONG: "We're out of that. Try again in a few days."

RIGHT: "It looks like that item will be back in the store on Tuesday. Would you like me to put one aside for you when it comes in? I'll give you a call when it's here and ready for you."

DON'T
make it the
CUSTOMER'S
FAULT

You work for a company that manufactures GPS devices. A customer writes you an e-mail saying she bought one because it was the only one she could find that was compatible with Macintosh computers, but that it went completely dead while she was hiking in unfamiliar territory. She brought it back to the store and got a new one, but that one also died two weeks later. She has returned the second one as well, but she wants you to know there may be a problem with the model in general.

WRONG: Respond in an e-mail to the customer, telling her that there have been no other records of that device failing. "It must be something you're doing. We have no other models that are Mac compatible, so there's nothing we can do for you."

RIGHT: "We are terribly sorry for the inconvenience, as we know that our customers rely on our products to help them find great trails and get home safely. We will look into the issue with this model. Thank you for bringing it to our attention."

DON'T ACCUSE OTHER EMPLOYEES

You work for a wireless service provider. A customer calls and tells you that a rep in one of the company's stores told him he would receive his new phone for a particular price, but when he received his credit card bill, he learnt he had been charged twice that amount. He had not checked his receipt in the store because the rep offered to e-mail it to him.

WRONG: "Yeah, the guys in the stores make things up. You should have checked your receipt before you left. You can't really believe what you hear in the stores."

RIGHT: "I'm terribly sorry for the confusion. If you don't mind waiting a moment, I'll research this and find out what price you were supposed to be charged."

DON'T
let a customer
GO AWAY
ANGRY

You work for a cosmetics company. A customer calls and says she tried using your newest hair color product, but it rinsed right out and didn't cover her gray hair at all.

WRONG: "Are you sure you used it correctly? That should have worked, so if it didn't, you probably didn't mix it right or leave it in long enough."

RIGHT: "I'm so sorry about that. I'll send a note to the product team with your feedback. Also, we want to make this up to you, so I will send you coupons for free products: You can try some of our other formulas and see if you have a better experience. Thank you so much for calling so we can make this right."

DON'T JUMP *to* CONCLUSIONS

You run a company that provides meeting facilitation services to businesses. After one such meeting, a client calls to complain about one of your facilitators. He says that your employee wasn't very well trained, and that the meeting did not go as well as it should have gone. He wants a credit on his bill.

WRONG: "Are you sure it was my employee's fault? Or did the meeting just not produce the result you wanted? That's not his fault—that's your problem with your organization."

RIGHT: "I'm very sorry to hear this. Tell me about the meeting, and where you feel it went wrong. I'll go back and talk to my employee so I have a full picture of the event, and we'll straighten this out. Thank you so much for letting me know about this."

DON'T BE MEAN

You run an advertising agency, and you make a big presentation for a client. He doesn't like any of your ideas, but can't specify why. All he says is, "I don't know, they just didn't do it for me. Go come up with some others."

WRONG: "Okay, it's your money. I can't see why you didn't like these concepts—maybe they're just too intellectual for you. You want something you don't have to think about so much."

RIGHT: "I'm sorry we disappointed you. It would be great to have more specifics on what you didn't like about these, so we can come back with a campaign that will hit the mark for you."

DON'T TRANSFER RESPONSIBILITY

You own an oil change and car maintenance business. One of your employees accidentally double-fills a customer's oil tank, and your customer calls from his home to tell you that blue smoke is rising from under his hood.

WRONG: "I don't know what the problem is, or if it even has anything to do with us. You'll have to bring the car back here somehow. Call for a tow truck."

RIGHT: "Wow, I am really sorry about this. I'll send one of my technicians out to your home right away, and we'll get the problem solved. Don't drive your car anywhere until we've checked it out and determined what the problem is."

DON'T GET DEFENSIVE,
even when you're right

You own a jewelry store, and a customer brings in an old watch to have you replace the crystal. In the course of working on it, your technician determines that it's in bad shape and cannot be repaired. As you remove the crystal, it cracks and breaks. When you give your customer the news, he accuses your store of breaking his watch.

WRONG: "This is one of the best jewelry stores in the area. Your watch was broken when it got here. There's nothing else I can do for you."

RIGHT: Involving an expert can defuse a bad situation quickly. "Our technician would be happy to talk with you about why the watch doesn't work and what happened to the crystal. Let me bring him out here to explain what happens to older watches like this one."

DON'T
talk with a
SHOUTING
CUSTOMER
in front of other customers

You are a manager in an appliance store. A customer comes in on a busy Saturday with a blender he bought the day before. He demands to speak to a manager about a problem with it. As you approach him, he immediately raises his voice to describe the malfunction. He gets angrier and starts shouting.

WRONG: "Sir, if you don't lower your voice, I'll have to ask you to leave the store."

RIGHT: "Sir, I have an office in back. Let's talk there." When you get there, continue with, "Sir, I will do whatever I can to make this right for you. Please have a seat, and tell me again what happened."

DON'T
BE TOO
LAZY
to make a sale

A customer calls your shoe store looking for a specific brand and style of shoe. An employee on the floor picks up the call.

WRONG: The employee doesn't bother to check. He just tells the customer, "We don't carry that." He hangs up without offering to order the item, or suggesting a substitute.

RIGHT: The employee checks to see if the item is on the shelf. If not, he checks inventory to see if it's in stock. When he finds that it is not, he says, "I would be happy to order that for you. We can have it here in three days. Would that fit your schedule? Okay, what size do you need?"

DON'T REFUSE
to connect to
YOUR
SUPERVISOR

You take a call from a customer who is upset about her wireless service. After less than a minute on the phone with you, she demands to speak to your supervisor.

WRONG: "No, I won't connect you with my supervisor. She can't do anything more for you than I can. You have to talk to me."

RIGHT: "I would be happy to connect you. First, can you give me all the details of your problem, so I can brief her before she speaks with you? I may even be able to help you myself and save you some time."

DON'T
TURN AWAY
a customer in
DISTRESS

It's 8 p.m., and your car dealership's service department closes at nine. You get a call from a woman who tells you she's from out of town and on a driving vacation with her family. Her car is making a terrible grinding noise, and she's hoping she can just drive over and have your technicians take a look at it.

WRONG: "I'm sorry, but we close in an hour. Even if you bring your car over, we'll have to keep it overnight. No one has time to look at it now."

RIGHT: "Of course, we are happy to help. If you can bring the car in right now, we'll test drive it with you and start to determine what's wrong. If you need to stay overnight in the area, I can call around and help you find a hotel while we're waiting to know for sure. Is there any other way I can help you this evening?"

DON'T
discuss your own
PROBLEMS

You are a server in a restaurant. A customer waves you down and asks why his order has not come yet. You check and find out the kitchen is backed up because of a large party ahead of your customer. You return to the table to explain.

WRONG: "This place is so screwed up! There's a big party ahead of you, so they haven't even started your order yet. Typical!"

RIGHT: "I'm so sorry for the wait. There's a large party ahead of you, but your order will be out shortly. In the meantime, may I bring you some additional bread, or an appetizer? The shrimp cocktail is already assembled, so I could bring each of you one of those right away if you're really hungry."

References

Aklap, Nellie. "4 Ways to Outdo Your Competitors." American Express OPEN Forum, April 14, 2012. Accessed February 27, 2015. http://mashable.com/2012/04/14/business-beat-competitors/.

Alessandra, Tony, PhD. "Assuring Customer Satisfaction." Accessed March 3, 2015. http://www.alessandra.com/freeresources/Assuring CustomerSatisfaction.asp.

Baird Group. "Service Recovery: 5 Steps For Making Things Right." Accessed March 2, 2015. http://baird-group.com/articles/service -recovery-5-steps-for-making-things-right.

Balle, Louise. "List of Customer Service Empathy Words." Smallbusiness .chron.com. Accessed March 3, 2015. http://smallbusiness.chron.com /list-customer-service-empathy-words-1126.html.

Basu, Abhiroop. "How to Satisfy Customers Using the Right Tone of Voice." Zendesk. February 10, 2015. Accessed March 1, 2015. https:// www.zendesk.com/blog/right-tone-of-voice.

Bhasin, Kim. "13 Epic Twitter Fails by Big Brands." Business Insider, February 6, 2012. Accessed March 19, 2015. http://www.businessinsider .com/13-epic-twitter-fails-by-big-brands-2012-2#.

Brown, Elliott. "7 Essential Steps to Solving Customer Service Problems with Content." SurveyMonkey Blog, August 4, 2014. Accessed March 19, 2015. https://www.surveymonkey.com/blog/en/blog/2014/08/04 /7-steps-better-customer-customer-service/.

Business Victoria. "Define and Know Your Customer." Accessed February 25, 2015. http://www.business.vic.gov.au/marketing-sales-and-online /increasing-sales-through-marketing/defining-and-knowing -your-customer.

Capterra. "Top Customer Loyalty Software Products." Accessed March 19, 2015. http://www.capterra.com/customer-loyalty-software/.

Chapman, Lisa. "How One Southwest Airlines Employee Delivered Exceptional Customer Service." Blog: Marketing and Social Media, July 2, 2010. Accessed March 18, 2015. http://managementhelp.org/blogs /marketing/2010/07/southwest-airlines-employee/.

Ciotti, Gregory. "15 Customer Service Skills that Every Employee Needs." Help Scout. February 20, 2013. Accessed March 18, 2015. http:// www.helpscout.net/blog/customer-service-skills/.

Ciotti, Gregory. "How to Handle 8 Challenging Customer Service Scenarios." HelpScout.net. Accessed March 6, 2015. http:// www.helpscout.net/blog/customer-service-scenarios/.

Ciotti, Gregory. "The Right (and Wrong) Way to Handle a Company Crisis." HelpScout, Nov. 18, 2013, Accessed March 17, 2015. http:// www.helpscout.net/blog/crisis-management-examples/.

Ciotti, Gregory. "Support Teams: Stop Being Blinded by Faster Response Times." Help Scout, March 5, 2014. Accessed March 18, 2015. https:// www.helpscout.net/blog/speed-kills/.

Conradt, Stacy. "11 of the Best Customer Service Stories Ever." Mental Floss, March 12, 2012. Accessed March 18, 2015. http://mentalfloss.com /article/30198/11-best-customer-service-stories-ever.

Conti, Connie. "10 Ways to Improve Your Inbound Call Center Greeting." The Connection Contact Center Services, October 30, 2013. Accessed February 27, 2015. http://www.the-connection.com/10-ways-to -improve-your-inbound-call-center-greeting/.

Customer Advocate. "Don't Call Me Mate: A Practical Guide on How to Address the Customer." Accessed March 1, 2015. http://www .thecustomeradvocate.co.uk/customer-service-training/call-mate -practical-guide-address-customer/.

Customer Lifecycle, LLC. "Get Better Business Results From the Four Stages of Your Customer Lifecycle: Stage 4—Retain." Accessed February 24, 2015. http://www.customerlifecycle.us/pdfs/clcwhitepapers /Get%20Better%20Business%20Results%20Retention.pdf.

DailyFinance.com. "Best and Worst Customer Service Stories." Accessed March 19, 2015. http://www.dailyfinance.com/photos/best-and-worst -customer-service/#!fullscreen&slide=987700.

Dampler, Phillip. "Charter Cable Tells Tornado Victims to 'Look Around the Neighborhood' for Cable Boxes or Else." Stop the Cap! May 16, 2011. Accessed March 17, 2015. http://stopthecap.com/2011/05/18/charter -cable-tells-tornado-victims-to-look-around-the-neighborhood-for -cable-boxes-or-else/.

Davis, Bonnie Jo. "Define Your Target Audience—Who Is Your Client?" SalesGravy. Accessed February 25, 2015. https://www.salesgravy.com /sales-articles/marketing/define-your-target-audience-who-is-your -client.html.

Default, Alice. "How to Talk to Your Customers in 6 Easy Steps." Accessed February 27, 2015. http://blog.frontapp.com/how-to-talk-to-your -customers-in-6-easy-steps/.

Dixon, Matthew, Karen Freeman, and Nicholas Toman. "Stop Trying to Delight Your Customers." *Harvard Business Review*. July 2010. Accessed March 18, 2015. https://hbr.org/2010/07/stop-trying-to-delight-your -customers.

Dun & Bradstreet. "What Traits Do Your Best Customers Share?" Accessed February 26, 2015. http://www.dnb.com/lc/sales-marketing -education/evaluating-a-customer.html#.VO-VNkL82Dg.

Edelman, Ben. "A Harvard Professor Found a $4 Difference on His Chinese Food Bill. And Then All Hell Broke Loose." FailBlog. December 5, 2014. Accessed March 17, 2015. http://failblog.cheezburger.com/tag /customer-service.

8X8, Inc. "Tips for Writing Your Auto Attendant Script." Accessed February 27, 2015. https://www.8x8.com/Resources/Learn/Hints-and -Tips/Auto-Attendant-Script-Writing-Tips.

Eley, Brandon. "When Customers Lie." SitePoint Business and Marketing. November 30, 2011. Accessed March 17, 2015. http://www.sitepoint.com /when-customers-lie/.

Elliott, Christopher. "Comcast Thinks My Husband Is an A**hole—and They Put It in Writing." Elliott.org. January 28, 2015. Accessed March 1, 2015. http://elliott.org/is-this-enough-compensation/comcast-thinks -husband-ahole-put-writing/.

Farrell, Bob. "The Pickle Principle." Give 'Em the Pickle.com. Accessed March 6, 2015. http://www.giveemthepickle.com/pickle_principle.htm.

Feloni, Richard. "The 10 Biggest Social Media Marketing Fails of 2013." Business Insider. November 24, 2013. Accessed March 20, 2015. http:// www.businessinsider.com/10-worst-social-media-marketing-fails-of -2013-2013-11.

Gallagher, Richard. *The Customer Service Survival Kit: What to Say to Defuse Even the Worst Customer Situations.* New York: AMACOM, 2013.

Garofalo, Steve. "The Three Stages of the Customer Experience." Quoteroller.com. April 29, 2014. Accessed February 24, 2015. http:// blog.quoteroller.com/2014/04/29/three-stages-customer-experience/.

Golden, Myra. "Top 6 Ways to Get an Angry Customer to Back Down." YouTube. April 5, 2007. Accessed March 7, 2015. https://www.youtube .com/watch?v=ACKbkmO9rLg&index=2&list=PLB9B0AFB9FB213135.

Holcomb, Mangan. "Verizon Wireless Giving Customers Extra GB of Data." Verizon Wireless news release. November 12, 2014. Accessed March 5, 2015. http://www.thv11.com/story/news/local/little-rock/2014/11/12 /verizon-wireless-giving-customers-extra-gb-of-data/18923175/.

Howe, Carol. "Consumers Will Drive iPhone Ownership Past Android's Peak." 451 Resarch Yankee Group. April 25, 2013. Accessed March 18, 2015. http://www.yankeegroup.com/ResearchDocument.do?id=60321.

Hsu, Tiffany. "Taco Bell Helicopters 10,000 Tacos to Bethel, Alaska, after Hoax." *Los Angeles Times*, July 3, 2012. Accessed March 18, 2015. http://www.latimes.com/business/la-fi-mo-taco-bell-alaska-20120703 -story.html.

Korte, Derek. " 'Giving Customers Options Can Improve Service (and Sales)': Joe Crisara." *Field Service Digital*. October 15, 2013. Accessed March 5, 2015. http://fieldservice.com/2013/10/15/giving-customers -options-can-improve-service-and-sales-joe-crisara/.

Laya, Patricia. "Nightmare: 7 Customer Service Blunders That Went Viral." Business Insider. June 17, 2011. Accessed March 17, 2015. http://www.businessinsider.com/7-very-public-lessons-in-customer-service-2011-6#.

Long, Jonathan. "Turn Prospects into Customers with These 8 Tips." Entrepreneur.com. September 8, 2014. Accessed March 2, 2015. http://www.entrepreneur.com/article/237130.

Male, Bianca. "8 Ways to Listen to Your Customers." Business Insider. June 2, 2010. Accessed March 2, 2015. http://www.businessinsider.com/8-ways-to-listen-to-your-customers-2010-6.

Marketing Tech Blog. "The New Rules of Customer Engagement for Marketing, Sales and Service." Accessed February 24, 2015. https://www.marketingtechblog.com/marketing-sales-service-new-rules-customer-engagement/.

Marshall, Perry. "The 80/20 Rule of Sales: How to Find Your Best Customers." Entrepreneur.com. October 9, 2013. Accessed February 26, 2015. http://www.entrepreneur.com/article/229294.

Mazza, Ed. "Comcast Apologizes after Changing Customer's Name to 'Asshole Brown.'" The Huffington Post, January 29, 2015. Accessed March 1, 2015. http://www.huffingtonpost.com/2015/01/29/comcast-asshole-brown_n_6568238.html.

Michalowicz, Mike. "7 Typical Lies Customers Tell Their Vendors." December 14, 2014. Accessed March 17, 2015. http://www.mikemichalowicz.com/7-typical-lies-customers-tell-vendors/.

Miller, Adrian. "7 Steps to Excellent Customer Service." Businessknowhow.com. Accessed March 18, 2015. http://www.businessknowhow.com/marketing/exceptional-customer-service.htm.

Minetor, Randi. How to Start a Home-Based Public Relations Business. Guilford, CT: Morris Book Publishing, 2012.

Moltz, Barry. "7 Ways to Master the Art of Business Follow-Up." Small Business Trends. October 8, 2013. Accessed March 2, 2015. http://smallbiztrends.com/2013/10/customer-follow-up.html.

Moore, Geoffrey. *Crossing the Chasm: Marketing and Selling High-Tech Products to Mainstream Customers,* Revised ed. New York: Harper Business Essentials, 1999.

Moran, Lee. "WestJet Airlines Surprises Passengers with Gifts after They Touch Down from Flights." *New York Daily News.* December 11, 2013. Accessed March 18, 2015. http://www.nydailynews.com/news/world /airline-surprises-passengers-christmas-gifts-article-1.1544292.

Murano, Grace. "Nine Awesome Customer Service Stories." Oddee. January 10, 2015. Accessed March 18, 2015. http://www.oddee.com /item_99200.aspx

Nasser, Kate. "The 25 Worst Customer Service Stories to Train the Best CSRs." Accessed March 12, 2013. http://katenasser.com/worst-customer -service-stories-train-best-csrs/.

Palmer, Kimberly. "10 Companies That Make Customers Happy." *US News & World Report.* October, 16, 2013. Accessed February 27, 2015. http:// money.usnews.com/money/personal-finance/articles/2013/10/16/10 -companies-that-make-customers-happy.

Phonepro.com. "Acknowledge, Then Take Action." August 27, 2013. Accessed March 3, 2015. http://www.phonepro.com/articles-more /acknowledge-action/.

Power, J.D. IV. "How to Really Listen to Your Customers." *Fast Company.* April 9, 2014. Accessed March 2, 2015. http://www.fastcompany.com /3028810/bottom-line/how-to-listen-really-listen-to-your-customers.

Ramshaw, Adam. "Case study: How to Apologize to Your Customers When Things Go Badly Wrong." Genroe. Accessed March 2, 2015. http:// www.genroe.com/blog/case-study-how-to-apologize-to-your-customers -when-things-go-badly-wrong/2493.

Robbins, David. "How Was It for Your Customer? Building Loyalty through Positive and Memorable Experiences." Gfk.com, February 18, 2015. Accessed March 19, 2015. http://blog.gfk.com/2015/02/how-was-it -for-your-customer-building-loyalty-through-positive-and-memorable -experiences/.

Root, George N., III. "Examples of Excellent Customer Service Skills." Chron Small Business. Accessed March 9, 2015. http://smallbusiness .chron.com/examples-excellent-customer-service-skills-2082.html.

Saliba, Chris. "Empathy Statements for Customer Service Representatives." CSM. Accessed March 3, 2015. http://www.customerservicemanager.com /empathy-statements-for-customer-service-representatives.htm.

Schied, Jean, and Marjorie Pilley. "Change How You Deal with Consumers to Gain Loyal Customers." Bright Hub. June 28, 2011. Accessed March 7, 2015. http://www.brighthub.com/office/human-resources/articles /120328.aspx.

Schofield, Jack. "Google Plus: Three Years Old and Still Failing as a Social Network." ZDnet.com. June 29, 2014. Accessed March 20, 2015. http:// www.zdnet.com/article/google-plus-three-years-old-and-still-failing -as-a-social-network/.

Solomon, Micah. "How to Think Like Apple about the Customer Service Experience." Forbes.com. November 21, 2014. Accessed March 1, 2015. http://www.forbes.com/sites/micahsolomon/2014/11/21/how-apple -thinks-differently-about-the-customer-service-experience-and-how -it-can-help-you/.

Spevak, Jeff. "Christopher Wilke's Lute Saga Continues." *Rochester Democrat & Chronicle*. January 23, 2014. Accessed February 24, 2015. http://www.democratandchronicle.com/story/lifestyle/2014/01/22 /christopher-wilkes-lute-saga-continues/4786373/?from=global &sessionKey=&autologin=.

Spevak, Jeff. "Delta Airlines repairs Christopher Wilke's lute." *Rochester Democrat & Chronicle*. November 13, 2014. Accessed February 24, 2015. http://www.democratandchronicle.com/story/lifestyle/music/2014 /11/12/delta-airlines-repairs-christopher-wilkes-lute/18929417/.

SpoutSocial. "The Social Business: Highlights from the Sprout Social Index." Accessed March 20, 2015. http://sproutsocial.com/insights /data/social-business-highlights-sprout-social-index/.

Stansburg, Glen. "10 Examples of Shockingly Excellent Customer Service." Open Forum, American Express. May 4, 2010. Accessed March 18, 2015. https://www.americanexpress.com/us/small-business/openforum/articles/10-examples-of-shockingly-excellent-customer-service-1/.

Steenkamp, Anneke. "6 Tips for Better Online Customer Support." ZopimBlog. April 9, 2014. Accessed March 20, 2015. https://blog.zopim.com/2014/04/08/6-tips-best-online-customer-support/.

Strategyn. "Who Is Your Customer? Accelerate Revenue Growth by Defining Customers Differently." Accessed February 25, 2015. https://strategyn.com/who-is-your-customer/.

Sun, Calvin. "10 Ways to Explain Things More Effectively." TechRepublic.com. April 1, 2008. Accessed March 4, 2015. http://www.techrepublic.com/blog/10-things/10-ways-to-explain-things-more-effectively/.

Tate, Ashley. "Top 10 Retail Loyalty Programs." The BigDoor Blog. December 11, 2013. Accessed March 19, 2015. http://bigdoor.com/blog/2013/12/11/top-10-retail-loyalty-programs/.

Taylor, David. "How Do You Treat Your Potential Customers?" A Working Website. June 2, 2011. Accessed February 27, 2015. http://aworkingwebsite.com/treat-potential-customers/.

VanSight. "When a Customer Demands to Speak to a Supervisor." Accessed March 4, 2015. http://www.slideshare.net/vansight/5-when-a-customer-demands-to-speak-with-your-supervisor.

Vogel, Amanda. "Setting Limits with Challenging Customers." Idealift.com. Accessed March 4, 2015. http://www.ideafit.com/fitness-library/setting-limits-with-challenging-customers.

Walter, Elizabeth. "10 Tips for Reputation and Crisis Management in the Digital World." *Forbes*. November 12, 2013. Accessed March 20, 2015. http://www.forbes.com/sites/ekaterinawalter/2013/11/12/10-tips-for-reputation-and-crisis-management-in-the-digital-world/.

Wharton School. "Getting to Wow': Consumers Describe What Makes a Great Shopping Experience." Knowledge @ Wharton. July 8, 2009. Accessed March 19, 2015. http://knowledge.wharton.upenn.edu/article

/getting-to-wow-consumers-describe-what-makes-a-great-shopping
-experience/.

White, Alan. "Here's What to Do If People Post Embarrassing Pictures
of You Online." BuzzFeed. September 7, 2014. Accessed March 20, 2015.
http://www.buzzfeed.com/alanwhite/heres-how-to-remove
-embarrassing-pictures-of-you-from-social#.qmxEz5Yol.

Williams, Donna. "Here's the Fastest Way to Outdo Your Competition."
Accessed February 27, 2015. http://www.evancarmichael.com
/Marketing/3931/Heres-the-fastest-way-to-outdo-your-competition
.html.

Wyse, Susan E. "5 Examples of Survey Demographic Questions."
Snap Surveys. March 13, 2012. Accessed February 25, 2013. http://www
.snapsurveys.com/blog/5-survey-demographic-question-examples/.

Yahoo Games. "Boy Writes Letter to Lego after Losing Minifigure, Gets
Awesome Response." January 8, 2013. Accessed March 18, 2015. https://
games.yahoo.com/blogs/plugged-in/boy-writes-letter-lego-losing
-minifigure-gets-awesome-220816003.html.

Index

A

Abrams, Rhonda, 85
Accidental lies, 152
Accounts receivable in
    limitations, 87
Accusations, making false, 285
Acknowledging, 76–78
    active listening in, 76, 77
    anger in customers, 77
    recognizing repeat customers, 78
    summarizing what you hear, 76
    visiblity of customer in, 78
Acquisition stage of customer
    services, 14
Actions, recording, 142
Active listening, 76, 77
Advertising
    on Instagram, 226
    resisting urge for, in inbound call
        greetings, 46
Affinity groups, finding, in attracting
    customers, 29
Airlines
    baggage handling by, 10–12,
        168, 208
    Twitter campaign of, 223
    Twitter use by, 240
Airplanes
    condensation leak on, 134
    unattended children on, 133
Airport Fast Park at the Baltimore-
    Washington Airport, 213
Alexandra, Tony, 74
Allergic reactions, 158
Alternatives, 94–95

choices in satisfying customers, 94
    fulfilling needs in, 95
    making offers and, 94
    offering, 67
    price of, 95
American Express, 6
Analogies in explanations, 83
Anger
    acknowledging, 77
    in customers, 106, 110, 116, 300
    meeting with kindness, 112
    out-of-control, 139
    in the showroom, 139
    social media and, 240
Angie's List, 64
Answers
    finding the, 101
    keeping customers waitng for,
        100
Apologizing, 43, 49, 68–70
    to entire customer base, 69
    promising never again, 70
    quickness in, 68
    saying you are sorry in, 68
    sincerity in, 70
    telling customer what happened
        in, 69
Appdator, 186
Apple, 6, 13, 54, 173, 184, 185
Argument, customer desire for, 111
AT&T, 91
Attractions, TripAdvisor reviews
    of, 232
Audience, locating social media, 233
Authority, hiding behind higher, 274

Automatic rewards, 193
Automobiles, defects in, 165
Avatar, building, in customer
    identification, 22

B

Bad days, handling, 131
Baggage handling
    by Delta Airlines, 10–12, 168
    by Southwest Airlines, 208
    by United Airlines, 168
Bait, taking the, 89
Bank of America, 170
Barnum, P. T., 17
Basics, applying the, 37
BestBuy Reward Zone program, 189
Best Western Rewards program, 189
Better, acting as if you are, 293
Better Business Bureau, 146
Big data, accessing, in customer
    identification, 21
Bills for deceased customers, 168
Birthdays, celebrating, 188
Blogging, 165
    finding bloggers, 229
    Google searching for sites on, 229
    sharing information in, 30
BMW, 203
Body language, in communication, 52
Boren, David, 249
BP, 70
Brand loyalty, rewarding, 186–193
    access in, 191, 193
    automatic rewards in, 193
    birthdays and special occasions
        in, 188
    creating hierarchy in, 189
    doubling of points in, 191
    expiration dates and, 188
    free merchandise in, 189
    giving customers choices, 186
    insider intel in, 190
    keeping program simple, 190

members-only offers in, 191
offers in, 187
online-only programs in, 193
record keeping in, 186
reward expirations in, 188
rewards for every purchase, 190
rewards for total purchases, 192
services as rewards in, 189
stinginess and, 187
thinking beyond merchandise
    in, 192
Brands, 9
Brief
    keeping inbound call
        greetings, 45
    for supervisor, 90
British Airways, Twitter use by, 240
Buffer, 165, 197
Business. *Also see* Repeat business
    choosing social media for,
        233–238
    closing down, 146
    knowing your, 183
Business attitudes, 35–37
    basics in, 37
    can-do attitude in empowing
        employees in, 36
    ethics in, 36
    every employee is in customer
        service, 35
    keeping it simple, 37
Business Knowhow (website), 176
Buyer's remorse, 74

C

Cakes, handling problem with
    message on, 132
California, rolling blackouts in, 171
Call centers
    employees at as bearers of bad
        news, 159
    power outage in, 158
Calming-down customers, 290

Can-do attitude in empowering employees, 36
Caring, and being genuine, 202
Carroll, Dave, 168
CashFootprint, 186
Changes, communication of, 262
Chapman, Lisa, 208
Charter Cable, 167
"Check is in the mail," 154
Checkout, asking questions during, 62
Children, unattended, 133
Choices in satisfying customers, 94
Clancy, J. R., 175
Clarification of issues, 89
Claritin, 214
Clients. *See* Customer(s)
Clues, getting, from past customers, 24
CNN, 257
Comcast, 49
Comedy Central's @Midnight, 257
Comment cards, 200
Comments boxes, social media as replacement for, 197
Communication
    of changes, 262
    with hard of hearing, 131
    parts of, 52
    twitter as two-way, 222
Company
    covering errors of, 277
    explaining policies of, 100
    fault of, 103
    presenting on LinkedIn, 227
    searching LinkedIn for, 30
Competence in breeding satisfaction, 198
Competition
    going to the, 154
    outdoing your, 32–34
        competing on service as opposed to price, 34
        distinguishing yourself in, 32

keeping promises in, 34
    making customer satisfaction your culture in, 33
    putting customers first in, 33
    respecting customers in, 33
    serving unmet needs in, 32
    threat to go to, 147
Complaints
    corralling the chronic, 84
    5 percent rule in, 85
    handling about staff, 86
    on products, 151
Concerns
    handling genuine, 273
    showing sincerity in, 75
Conclusions, jumping to, 301
Connection, making a
    being pleasant and personable, 178
    learning likes, 180
    noticing details, 179
    recordkeeping in, 181
    remembering drink orders, 179
    remembering names in, 178
    thinking about customers, 180
Control freaks, 147
Courtesy, 203
    addressing problems with, 36
Coworkers, rudeness in, 157
Credits, denial of, 283
Crisara, Joe, 94
Crisis management
    actions not to take, 160–162
    anger in, 139–142
    complaints in, 156–159
    getting worse in, 163–164
    lies in, 152–155
    real-life crises in, 165–171
    sarcasm and threats in, 145–151
    unreasonable demands in, 143–144
Crossing the Chasm (Moore), 13
Crum, Kristi, 91
Customer(s)
    accident of, 129
    accusing of lying, 276

addressing, 47–49
  gender and, 48
  ma'am or miss?, 48
  showing respect, 47
  using customer's title in, 48
  using person's name, 47
anger in, 106, 110, 116, 300
apologizing to, 43
asking for referrals, 31
being available to, 195
bill for dead, 168
bringing of problem to your
    attention, 109
choices in satisfying, 94
communicating with
    forums, 236
complaining, 56
converting prospects to, 60–61
defusing anger in, 300
desire for argument, 111
desire to tell you how to
    do job, 106
dislike for being on hold, 123
in distress, 156
drunken, 163
gathering demographics on, 22
getting clues from past, 24
giving choices, 186
giving explanation to, 69
great service according to, 56
helping, 98, 295, 296
helping help others, 203
hurried, 110
immediate needs of, 120
impatience in, 99
inavailability of favorite
    items, 116
in-person versus telephone, 122
insults from angry, 106
interrogation of, 261
introducing, to new ideas, 196
keeping waiting for answer, 100
knowledge of internal
    processes, 268

learning likes of repeat, 180
length of time of service with
    angry, 110
looking at current, in customer
    identification, 21
losses of, 275
making contact easy, 63
making eye contact with, 260
making feel like deadbeats, 284
making of scenes by, 140
making their fault, 298
making visible, 78
micromanagement of, 269
missing of information and, 123
not-letting go of subject, 107, 144
offering quiet discretion to, 164
panic in, 108
passing around of, 111
plus-size, 104, 107, 278
potential (*See* Potential
    customers)
problems with previous, 117
putting first, 33
receipt of broken product, 104
recognizing repeat, 78
reminding on security, 233
respecting your, 33
self-importance of, 145, 148
selling best items for, 119
sending e-mail to, 247
showing commitment to, 196
social media and, 219
stranded, 105
taking of wrong steps by, 108
talking about experiences of, 204
talking with shouting, 305
telling what to do, 161
thanking for alerting you to
    problem, 80
thinking about, in building
    repeat business, 180
threatening of violence by, 140
traits of best, 26
treating as best friends, 55

treating employees as, 176
treating poorly, 75, 288
trying to calm down, 290
turning away distressed, 308
turning away for not following
	rules, 294
using earned title of, 48
using name of, 47
value of surveys in
	identifying, 62
wait for meal, 124
wants of, 27
warning about expiring
	rewards, 188
willingness to spend for better
	service, 55
wrong, 105
Customer attraction, 28–31
affinity groups in, 29
asking for referrals, 31
attending trade shows in, 28
building reputation for
	quality in, 30
sponsoring appropriate
	events in, 29
working the web in, 30
Customer base
apologizing to entire, 69
maintaining your, 16
Customer Contact Council, 184
Customer identification, 20–22
accessing big data in, 21
building avatar, 22
customer wants in, 27
defining target audience in, 23
80/20 rule in, 26
finding decision-maker in, 25
gathering demographics in, 22
getting clues from past
	clients, 24
looking at current customers, 21
problem solving in, 25
product offerings in, 20
purchasing department in, 24

research in, 20
R-F-M rule in, 27
surveys in, 21, 62
taking survey in, 21
traits of best customers in, 26
Customer satisfaction, making your
	culture, 33
Customer service
acquisition stage of, 14
commitment to, 60
including all employees in, 35
a potent differentiator, 17
preparing question-and-answer
	document in, 247
retention stage of, 16–17
secret to, 6
serving stage of, 15–16
thinking about
	according to the
		customer, 56
	being grateful for
		complaining customers, 56
	costs of better, 55
	customers as best friends, 55
	experience in, 54
	making it easy, 57
	training employees to be
		experts, 57
whole product and, 12–13
CVS, 215

D

Data, accessing big, in customer
	identification, 21
Deadbeats, making customers feel
	like, 284
Dead bodies in hotel rooms, 163
Debtors' Revolt, launching on
	YouTube, 170
Decision-makers, finding, in
	customer identification, 25
Defensiveness, 304
about small things, 279

Delivery
    botched, 125
    handling late, 99
Delta Airlines, baggage handling
    by, 10–12, 168
Demands
    endless, 144
    unreasonable, 143–144
Demographics, gathering, in
    customer identification, 22
Denial
    of credits or refunds, 283
    of errors, 280
Details, noticing, 179
Digg (website), 230
Disappointment, turning, into
    frustration, 263
Discounted service, 113
Discounts, new customer, 148
Discretion, offering, 164
Dismissal, of others' plans, 282
Distress
    customers in, 156
    turning away customer in, 308
Drink orders, remembering, 179

E

Education, self-acquired, 17
Effort, making the, 202
80/20 rule, in customer
    identification, 26
Elderly, shaming the, 267
E-mail. *See also* Social media
    finishing with a question, 44
    sending to customers, 247
Empathy, 79–80, 108
    in answering telephone
        call, 53
    being sorry in, 80
    making personal connection
        in, 79
    saying I understand in, 79
    thanks in, 80
    words in, 79

Employees
    accusing other, 299
    defining limits for, 86
    empowering, 36
    giving needed time to resolve
        issue, 177
    giving needed tools, 177
    including all in customer
        service, 35
    investing in your, 174–177
        developing a service
            culture, 175
        emulating the right
            examples, 174
        getting everyone on the
            same page, 175
        giving employees needed
            time to resolve issue, 177
        giving employees needed
            tools, 177
        responsibility for excellent
            service, 176
        sharing stories internally, 174
        treating employees like
            customers, 176
    rudeness in, 135
    training to be experts, 57
    treating, like customers, 176
Employers, taking controversial
    stand by, 164
Empowerment of employees, 36
Endless demands, 144
Errors
    covering company, 277
    denial of, 280
    in an order, 114
Escalations, 286
Estate executors, 109
Ethics, importance of, 36
Ethnic slurs, 142
Events, sponsoring appropriate, in
    attracting customers, 29
Examples, emulating the right, 174
Expectations, setting of, 115

Experience, thinking about the, 54
Expertise, 129
Experts, training employees to be, 57
Expiration dates, 188
Explanations, 81–83
    analogies in, 83
    asking questions in, 83
    avoiding talking down in, 82
    being grateful for questions, 82
    bridging perception gap and, 81
    keeping simple, 81
Extra, giving little, 98
Eye contact, making with
    customers, 260

F

Facebook, 64, 137, 227. *See also*
    Social media
    getting video removed from, 246
    message cycle on, 256
    need to be on, 233
    negative comments on, 241
    online monitoring of, 234
    opinions on, 240
    posting guidelines for page, 241
    reasons for being on, 225
    sharing information on, 30
    takeoff of, 227
False accusations, making, 285
FAQs, maintaining list of, 237
Farrell, Bob, 98
Fat-shaming, 104, 107, 166, 278
Fault, making of customers, 298
Feedback
    asking for, 197
    looking for, on Yelp, 231
Felipe, Jay, 242
Firestone, 9
First, being, 156
5 percent rule in complaints, 85
Floorwalkers, 182
Following up, 71–73, 194
    begining with after the sale, 71
on issues, 72
    jumping on problem in, 73
    keeping track in, 72
    making special offers, 71
    in prospect conversion, 61
    sending note in, 73
    speaking to supervisor
        and, 88
    by telephone, 75
Ford Motor, 9, 146
Forms, filling out complex, 160
Forums in social media, 235, 236
FourSquare, 234
    checking, 228
Friendliness, 198
Friends, treating customers
    as best, 55
Frustration, turning
    disappointment into, 263

G

Gaylord Opryland Hotel, 209
Gender, guessing the, 48
Genesys, 195
Genius Bars, 185
Genroe strategic planning, 69
Gfk research firm, 199, 200
Gifts, 91–93
    damaged, 125
    healing slight with, 92
    holiday, 92
    loyalty and, 91
    using partnerships and, 92
    waiving of upcharge and, 93
Gift wrapping, 201
Giveaways, usefulness of, 93
Google+, 234
    reaching fringes on, 227
Google Alerts, 239
Google searches, 17, 30, 67, 229
*Gordon Ramsay's Kitchen
    Nightmares*, 240
Grateful, being, for questions, 82

Great Harvest Bread
    Company, 192
Greetings in inbound call
    greetings, 46
Groupons, 113

H

Hannum, David, 17
Hard of hearing, communicating
    with, 131
Harley-Davidson, 184
Hashtags, 222, 224
Hayward, Tony, 70
Hearing, 76. *See also* Listening
    summaring, 76
Help
    for customers, 295, 296
    making effort to, 182–183
        finding products in, 182
        floorwalkers in, 182
        knowing business and
            inventory, 183
    offering to, 88
Hierarchy, creating, in reward
    program, 189
HMV, 243
Honesty, addressing problems
    with, 36
HootSuite, 234
Hotel(s)
    emergency checkout at, 130
    jostled baggage at, 130
    late check-in at, 128
    TripAdvisor reviews of, 232
Hotel employees, handling illegal
    requests, 162
Hotel rooms
    dead body in, 163
    dirty, 127
    unserviced, 127
HowSociable, 234
Huffington Post, 257
Hypocrisy, 176
Hyundai, 203

I

Ideas, introducing customers to
    new, 196
Imbecile, treating customers
    like, 288
Impatience in customers, 99
Inbound call greetings, 45–46
    editing your script, 46
    keeping brief, 45
    providing route to real person, 46
    using consistent language in, 45
Information
    helping customer with, 98
    missing of, for customers, 123
    providing for prospect, 40
Insider intel, 190
Instagram
    advertising on, 226
    message cycle on, 256
    video removal from, 250
    as visual medium, 226
Internal processes, customer lack of
    knowledge of, 268
Internal Revenue Service, calls to, 57
Internet. *See also* Social media;
    Websites
    content on, 255
    message cycle on, 256
    message strategy on, 257
    viruses and, 255
Interrogation of customers, 261
Inventory, knowing your, 183
Invoice, receipt of incorrect, 113
IP.Board, 236
Issues
    clarification of, 89
    following up on, 72
    giving employees needed time
        to resolve, 177
Items
    botched delivery of, 125
    burial of, in stock room, 118
    inavailability of favorite, 116

locating lost, 120
not in stock, 118
problems with, 134
selling best, for customer, 119
unavailability of, 102
wrong price on, 121

J

JetBlue People Officer, 211
Jobs, Steve, 54
Johnson & Johnson, 169
J.P.Morgan Chase, 244

K

Kindle Fire HDX tablet, 209
Kindness, meeting anger with, 112
King, Chris, 210
Kmart, robo-responses and, 243
Knowledge, lack of, 287

L

Language
    body, in communication, 52
    using consistent in inbound call
        greetings, 45
    using simple, 42
Laziness, 291
    in making sale, 306
Lee, Jimmy, 244
Lego Customer Service, 207
Levitt, Steven, 212
Lexus, 210
Libel, Twitter and, 254
Lies
    accidental, 152
    accusing customers of
        telling, 276
    of customers, 152–155
Life Alert, 204
Limitations, 84–87
    accounts receivable in, 87

being wary of special favors, 85
corralling the chronic
    complainer, 84
defining for employees, 86
5 percent rule in, 85
handling complaints about
    staff, 86
LinkedIn, 234
    presenting company on, 227
    searching for company names
        on, 30
Listening, 205
    active, 76, 77
    at checkout, 62
    creation of online
        communities, 63
    making it easy for customers to
        contact you, 63
    time limits and, 63
    truth and, 64
    value of surveys and, 62
    to your mother, 41
Live chats, 235, 238
    waiting for, 234
Lost items, locating, 120
Loyalty
    brand (*See* Brand loyalty,
        rewarding)
    building customer, 173–215
        going beyond the extra mile,
            206–215
        investing in people, 174–177
        making a connection in,
            178–181
        making effort to help,
            182–185
        rewarding brand loyalty,
            186–193
        through great service, 194–205
    building through service,
        194–205
        being in love, 198
        being memorable, 200, 201

being there for the customer, 195
comment cards and surveys, 200
competence in breeding satisfaction, 198
courtesy in, 203
creating memorable experience, 199
customer experiences in, 204
demonstrations in, 196
effort in, 202
feedback in, 197
following up in, 194
genuine caring in, 202
getting out and, 204
gift wrapping, 201
giving regulars a little extra, 195
helping customers help others, 203
introducing customers to new ideas, 196
making positive memory, 199
pleasure in, 203
recognizing and correcting problems, 197
saying thanks, 195
sitting and listening, 205
taking to heart, 205
thank-you card in, 194
surprises in leading to, 91
The Loyalty Box, 186
Loyalty cards, access to, 191
LoyaltyGator, 186
Loyalty programs
of BestBuy, 189
of Best Western, 189
keeping simple, 190
of Neiman Marcus, 189
online, 193
of Red Roof Inn, 193
of Starbucks, 189
of Victoria's Secret, 186

Lunch, getting a free, 153

M

Ma'am, use of, 48
Macy's, 202
Manager, telling the, 146
Meal, waiting, for in restaurant, 124
Meanness, 302
Media, calling the, 149
Mehrabian, Albert, 52
Members-only offers, 191
Memorable experiences, creating, 199, 200, 201
Memory, characteristics of positive, 199
Merchandise, thinking beyond, 192
Messages, controlling, 165
Michigan, University of, Population Studies Center, as information source, 21
Micromanagement, of patrons, 269
Mile, going beyond the extra, 206–215
    Airport Fast Park at the Baltimore Washington Airport and, 213
    CVS and, 215
    Gaylord Opryland Hotel and, 209
    JetBlue and, 211
    Kindle Fire HDX tablet and, 209
    Legos and, 207
    Lexus and, 210
    Mortons and, 214
    Nordstrom and, 206, 210
    poison control and, 214
    restroom save in, 208, 221
    Ritz-Carlton and, 213
    Sainsbury's and, 210
    Southwest Airlines and, 208
    Starbucks and, 206
    Taco Bell and, 215
    Trader Joe's and, 212
    United Airlines and, 212
    WestJet Airlines and, 207

Zappos and, 211
Miller, Adrian, 176
Minch, Ann, 170
Mistakes, owning the, 67, 165
Moore, Geoffrey, 13
Morton's, 214
Mother, listening to your, 41
MySpace, checking out pop culture on, 231
Mystery problems, 112

N

Names, remembering, 178
National Foundation for Credit Counseling, 154
Natural greeting, in answering telephone call, 51
Needs
    fulfillment of, 95
    serving unmet, 32
Neiman Marcus's InCircle program, 189
New customer discounts, 148
Nordstrom, 210
    extra service at, 206
Notes, sending, in following up, 73

O

Offers, 187
    to help, 88
    making, 94
    members-only, 191
    special, 191
    updating or modifying, 205
Online communities, creating, 63
Online-only programs, 193
Opinions, on Facebook, 240
Orders
    errors in, 114
    slowness in coming, 115
Outdated warranties, 119
Out-of-control anger, 139
Overbearing parents, 133

Overpromising, 66, 185

P

Package, disappearance of, 121
Packaging, tamper-proof, 169
Page, getting everyone on same, 175
Panera Bread, 186, 187
Panic in customers, 108
Parents, overbearing, 133
Partnerships, giveways and, 92
Parts, missing, 157
Passing around of customers, 111
Passwords, guarding, 243
Patience, loss of, 266
Patient, giving information to family of, 124
Patronizing behavior, 145
Pay, not going to, 149
People with disabilities, sensitivity with, 271
Perception gap, briding, 81
Perfection, pursuit of, 74
Person
    providing route to, in inbound call greetings, 46
    using name of, 47
Personable, being, 178
Personal connection, making, in showing empathy, 79
Personalized, face-to-face service, 209
Photos on Pinterest, 230
phpBB, 236
Pickle Principle, 98
Pinterest
    online monitoring of, 234
    photos on, 230
    sharing information on, 30
    takeoff of, 227
Pleasant, being, 178
Plus-size customers, 104, 107, 278
Poison control, 214
Policy, sticking to, 289

Pop culture, checking on
    Myspace, 231
Potential customers
    capturing prospect
        information, 39
    first impressions and, 38
    following up with prospects, 39
    keeping in touch, 40
    making prospects feeling
        important, 38
    providing information to be used
        by prospect, 40
    responding to prospects, 39
Power outage
    in call center, 158
    as not the power company's
        fault, 170
    as power company's fault, 171
Preferred Market Solutions, 186
Prescriptions, incorrect, 169
Price
    competition on service versus, 34
    offering of alternatives, 95
    wrong, on items, 121
Proactive, being about problems, 67
Problems
    being proactive about, 67
    bring to your attention, 109
    discussing, 309
    jumping on, 73
    recognizing and correcting, 197
Problem solving
    courtesy and honesty in, 36
    in customer identification, 25
    refusals in, 272
    social media and, 238
Product, fit of sales pitch to, 60
Products
    complaints on, 151
    in customer identification, 20
    receipt of broken, 104
    returning used, 155
Profanity, 141

Professional associations, as source
    of information, 20
Programs, online-only, 193
Promises
    avoiding over, 66
    delivering on, 184
    keeping your, 34, 66
Prospects
    asking questions of, 61
    capturing information on, 39
    conversion of, 60–61
    fit of sale pitch to product or
        service to, 60
    following up with, 39
    follow up in, 61
    keeping in touch with, 40
    providing information for, 40
    responding to, 39
    return on investment in, 61
    standing out in, 60
    web in, 60
Public relations, need for crisis
    plan, 249
Purchases
    rewards for every, 190
    rewards for total, 192

Q

Qantas Airlines, Twitter campaign
    of, 223
Quality, building reputation for, 30
Question-and-answer document, pre-
    paring in customer service, 247
Questions
    asking, in prospect conversion, 61
    asking during checkout, 62
    asking in explanations, 83
    being grateful for, 82
    finishing e-mail with a, 44

R

Racial slurs, 142
Ramshaw, Adam, 69

Reassuring, 74–75
  avoiding foolishness in, 75
  buyer's remorse in, 74
  following up by phone, 75
  forgotten training in, 74
  pursuit of perfection in, 74
  showing sincerity in, 75
Records
  keeping excellent, 181
  keeping good, 186
Reddit, 230
Red Roof Inn's loyalty program, 193
Referrals, asking for, 31
Refunds, denial of, 283
Refusals, in problem solving, 272
Regulars, giving extra to, 195
Rental reservations, 126
Repairs, complicated, 126
Repeat business
  learning likes and, 180
  recognizing customers in, 78
  thinking about customers in, 180
Repetition, eliminating, in inbound
    call greetings, 46
Reputation, building, for quality, 30
Requests
  dangerous, 162
  illegal, 162
  outrageous, 143
Research
  in customer identification, 20
  into target market, 19, 20
Respect, showing, for
    customers, 33, 47
Responsibility
  denial of, 264
  putting on others, 297
  transferal of, 303
Restaurants
  errors in order at, 114
  order not coming, 115
  remembering drink orders
      and, 179
  slow service in, 114

spiders in, 132
TripAdvisor reviews of, 232
waiting for meal in, 124
Restroom save on Twitter, 208, 221
Retention stage of customer
    services, 16–17
Return on investment (ROI) in
    prospect conversion, 61
Rewards
  automatic, 193
  creating hierarchy in, 189
  for every purchase, 190
  for total purposes, 192
  warning customer on expiring, 188
R-F-M rule in customer
    identication, 27
Right, making it
  avoiding overpromises, 66
  being proactive about
      problems, 67
  keeping promises, 66
  offering alternatives, 67
  owning the mistake, 65
  responding to social media, 65
Ritz-Carlton, 6, 54, 173
  customer service at, 213
River Cities, 186
Robo-responses, 243
Rolling blackouts, 171
Ronald MacDonald House
    Charities, 207
Rudeness
  in coworkers, 157
  in employees, 135
Rules
  bending of, 270
  request to break, 103
  turning away for not following, 294

S

Sainbury's, 210
Sales
  following up on, 71
  laziness and, 306

Sales pitch, fit of, to product or service, 60
Sarcasm, 145–151
Satisfaction, competence in breeding, 198
Scams, recognzing, 153
Schematics, posting on social media, 237
Schering-Plough, 214
Script
    editing, for inbound call greetings, 46
    going beyond, in answering telephone call, 51
Security, reminding customers on, 233
Self-acquired education, 17
Self-asertion, promoting, 150
Self-important customers, 148
Selling point, great service as a, 55
Sensei Wu, 207
Sensitivity, with people with disabilities, 271
Sephora, 191
Service
    building loyalty through, 194–205
        being in love, 198
        being memorable, 200, 201
        being there for the customer, 195
        comment cards and surveys, 200
        competence in breeding satisfaction, 198
        courtesy in, 203
        creating memorable experience, 199
        customer experiences in, 204
        demonstrations in, 196
        effort in, 202
        feedback in, 197
        following up in, 194
        genuine caring in, 202
        getting out and, 204
        gift wrapping, 201
        giving regulars a little extra, 195
        helping customers help others, 203
        introducing customers to new ideas, 196
        making positive memory, 199
        pleasure in, 203
        recognizing and correcting problems, 197
        saying thanks, 195
        sitting and listening, 205
        taking to heart, 205
        thank-you card in, 194
    competition on, versus price, 34
    discounted, 113
    fit of sales pitch to, 60
    responsibility for excellent, 176
    slowness of, 114, 115
    willinging of customers to spend for more, 55
Service culture, developing, 175
Serving stage of customer services, 15–16
Shaming of the elderly, 267
Shankman, Peter, 214
Shares, sharing internally, 174
Showroom, anger in the, 139
Sigma Alpha Epsilon, racist crisis for, 249
Simple
    keeping explanation, 81
    keeping things, 37
Simple language, using, 42
Slang, skipping the, 41
Slurs, racial or ethnic, 142
Smiling, when answering telephone call, 51
Smith, Kevin, 166
Snopes.com, 17, 245

Social media. *See also* Blogging;
    Facebook; FourSquare; Google+;
    Instagram; LinkedIn; MySpace;
    Pinterest; Reddit; TripAdvisor;
    Tumblr; Twitter; Yelp
  anger and, 240
  audience in, 233
  being consistent across
    channels, 236
  choosing, for your business,
    233–238
  customers and, 219
  forums in, 235, 236
  guarding passwords, 243
  live chats in, 234, 235, 238
  maintaining list of FAQs, 237
  messing up, 242–254
  as minefield of missteps, 217
  online monitoring tools in, 234
  opinions on, 240
  paying attention and, 239
  posting schematics and, 237
  power of, 12
  problem solving and, 238
  as replacement for Comments
    boxes, 197
  responding to, 67
  robo-responses and, 243
  security concerns for, 233
  setting and keeping hours on, 240
  strategy in using, 239
  tone-deafness and, 244
  as 24/7/365, 221
  waiting time in, 234
Sons of Maxwell, 168
Sony PlayStation Network, hacking
    of, 167
Sorry, saying you are, 68
Southwest Airlines, 6, 173, 201
  baggage handling by, 208
  fat passengers on, 166
Special favors, being wary of, 85
Special occasions, celebrating, 188

Special offers, 191
  making, in following up, 71
Spiders in restaurant, 132
Sprint, 91
Staff, handling complaints
    about, 86
Starbucks, 192
  handing out of store credit by, 206
  loyalty program of, 189
Stinginess, 187
Stock room, burial of items in, 118
Stop The Cap!, 167
Stores, servicing of customer at, 128
StumbleUpon, 230
Suggestions, welcoming, 42
Suit, threatening of, 147
Summarizing what you hear, 76
Supervisors
  refusal to connect to, 307
  speaking to, 88–90
    briefing in, 90
    clarification of issue, 89
    doctor asked me to call in, 90
    follow up in, 88
    offering to help, 88
    taking of bait in, 89
  unavailability of, 101
SurveyMonkey, 200
Surveys, 200
  in customer identification, 21, 62
Swearing, 141
  avoiding, 265

T

Taco Bell, 215
Taj Mumbai, Terrorists at, 166
Talking down, 82
Tamper-proof packaging, 169
Target audience, defining, 23
Target market, researching
    your, 19, 20
Telephone

bill for dead customer, 168
  following up by, 75
  inbound call greetings for, 45–46
Telephone calls
  answering, 50
  empathy in answering, 53
  going beyond script in, 51
  handling, versus in person
    customer, 122
  keeping track of, 72
  matching tone and speaking
    style, 52
  natural greeting in answering, 51
  rehearsing most used phrases, 53
  smiling when answering, 51
  timing in picking up, 50
  tone in answering, 50–53
  transfer of, 281
  unending, 117
Terrorists at Taj Mumbai, 166
Tesco Mobile, 242
Thanks, saying, 195
Thank-you cards, 194
Threats, 145–151
360Incentives.com, 186
Timberlake, Justin, 231
Time limits, avoiding, 63
T-Mobile, 91
Tone-deafness, 244
Tone in answering telephone
  calls, 50–53
Tools, giving employees needed, 177
Tosh 2.0, 255
Touch, keeping in, 40
Toyota, 146, 165
Tracking calls, 72
Trader Joe's, 198, 212
Trade shows, attending, in attracting
    customers, 28
Training, forgotten, 74
Transferal of responsibility, 303
TripAdvisor, 231
Trust, building, 184–185
  delivering on promise, 184

making it easy in, 184
  overpromising as problem in, 185
Truth, 64
Tumblr, 234
  going multimedia with, 228
Tweetdeck, 234
TweetReach, 234
24/7/365 universe, 221
Twitter, 137
  coordination of messages in, 223
  DM (direct message) with, 246
  fat-shaming and, 166
  following others on, 220
  getting alerts from, 225
  hashtags and, 222, 224
  learning how to use, 218
  libel and, 254
  lingering of mistakes in, 224
  making fast start with, 219
  need to be on, 233
  140-character limit in, 64, 223
  online monitoring of, 234
  problem solving and, 197
  reaching out to customers in, 251
  responding to security breach
    in, 165
  restroom save on, 208, 221
  searching for keywords on, 248
  sharing information on, 30
  stopping the lie on, 252, 253
  takeoff of, 227
  tweeting on, 122, 220
  as two-way communication, 222
  video removal from, 252
Tylenol Extra Strength, 169

U

Unavailability of item, 102
United Airlines
  baggage handling by, 168
  customer service of, 212
U.S. Bureau of Labor Statistics, as
    information source, 21

U.S. Census Bureau, as information source, 21
Unmet needs, serving, 32
Upcharge, waiving of, 93
Used returns, 155

V

vBulletin, 236
Verde Group, 204
Verizon Wireless, 91
Victoria's Secret, Loyalty program of, 186
Video
    damage control and, 251
    incriminating, 248
    removal from Facebook, 246
    removal from Instagram, 250
    removal from Twitter, 252
    removal from YouTube, 250
Vindictiveness, 292
Virgin Trains, 208, 221
Virus, 255
Visibility of customers, 78
Voice self-service, 195
Volume, 102

W

Waiting, responding to, 260
Walgreens, 169, 192
Waller, Fats, 56
Warranties, outdated, 119
Websites
    in converting prospect to customer, 60
    posting statement on, 253
    working, in attracting customers, 30

Wegmans supermarket, 182, 196
Weiner, Anthony, use of Twitter, 224
WestJet Airlines, 207
Whole product, customer services and, 12–13
Wilke, Christopher, 10–12
Word choice, 41–44
    apologizing and, 43
    in empathy, 79
    finishing with a question, 44
    genuineness in, 43
    listening to mother in, 41
    simplicity in, 42
    skipping the slang in, 41
    welcoming suggestions, 42
WordPress, 234

Y

Yelp, 64
    looking for feedback on, 231
YouTube, 137, 168, 207, 234
    "Debtors' Revolt" on, 170
    message cycle on, 256
    video removal from, 250

Z

Zappos, 211
Zooz Solutions, 186

93711578R00185

Made in the USA
Columbia, SC
13 April 2018